A Parents' Guide to Grading and Reporting

A Parents' Guide to Grading and Reporting

Being Clear about What Matters

Matt Townsley
Chad Lang

ROWMAN & LITTLEFIELD
Lanham • Boulder • New York • London

Published by Rowman & Littlefield
An imprint of The Rowman & Littlefield Publishing Group, Inc.
4501 Forbes Boulevard, Suite 200, Lanham, Maryland 20706
www.rowman.com

86-90 Paul Street, London EC2A 4NE, United Kingdom

Copyright © 2023 by Matt Townsley and Chad Lang

All rights reserved. No part of this book may be reproduced in any form or by any electronic or mechanical means, including information storage and retrieval systems, without written permission from the publisher, except by a reviewer who may quote passages in a review.

British Library Cataloguing in Publication Information Available

Library of Congress Cataloging-in-Publication Data

Names: Townsley, Matt author. | Lang, Chad, author.
Title: A parents' guide to grading and reporting : being clear about what matters / Matt Townsley and Chad Lang.
Description: Lanham, MD : Rowman & Littlefield, [2023] | Includes bibliographical references and index. | Summary: "Dr. Matt Townsley and Dr. Chad Lang have written a practical guide aimed at helping parents understand the ins and outs of grading and assessment in the 21st century"—Provided by publisher.
Identifiers: LCCN 2023019664 (print) | LCCN 2023019665 (ebook) | ISBN 9781475868012 (cloth) | ISBN 9781475868029 (paperback) | ISBN 9781475868036 (epub)
Subjects: LCSH: Grading and marking (Students)—United States. | Education—Parent participation—United States.
Classification: LCC LB3060.37 .T68 2023 (print) | LCC LB3060.37 (ebook) | DDC 371.27/20973—dc23/eng/20230510
LC record available at https://lccn.loc.gov/2023019664
LC ebook record available at https://lccn.loc.gov/2023019665

To my children, Caleb, Tyler, Nathan, and Keely. You have taught me so much about being a better parent and educator. This book is also dedicated to my own parents, Mike and Diane Townsley. Mom and Dad, you modeled the aims of this book for me as a child well before the 21st century. —Matt Townsley

To my children, Landon and Lauren, to whom I want to extend my heartfelt gratitude. Your presence in my life inspires me to be the best role model I can be and to always strive for excellence. Your future opportunities drive me to work toward making the world a better place for your success and that of others. I encourage you to always believe in yourselves and your abilities, to stay humble and curious, and to make a difference in the world. Thank you for being a constant source of motivation and inspiration. —Chad Lang

Contents

Foreword	ix
Acknowledgments	xi
Introduction	xiii
Chapter 1: Help!: Why Does My Child's Gradebook and Report Card Look Different than When I Was In School?	1
Chapter 2: But the Old Grading System Worked for Me: Why Are Schools Changing the Way They Grade?	17
Chapter 3: How Does 21st-Century Grading Hold My Child Accountable for Learning?	33
Chapter 4: What About College?: How Do These Grading Practices Affect GPA, Scholarships, and Post-High School Positioning?	49
Chapter 5: How Can I Partner with My Child's School in Grading and Feedback?	59
References	73
Index	79
About the Authors	83

Foreword

There are many partners in each child's education—teachers, support staff, administrators, peers, and, of course, their parents or guardians. As educators, we often say how important the partnership with parents is but then give only lip service to fostering that partnership by doing very little to help parents to understand what is happening in the classroom and, even more importantly, the *why* of what is happening in the classroom. A critically important part of the partnership with parents is the communication of learning but there have been very few attempts by educators to comprehensively explain to parents the *what* and *why* of grading and reporting. The only books of which I'm aware that attempted to do this were written by Rick Stiggins in 1997 and Tom Guskey in 2003, so to say that Matt Townsley and Chad Lang's book is long overdue and greatly needed is a huge understatement.

Professor Christopher Dede of the Harvard Graduate School of Education wrote in 1997 that *"The most dangerous experiment we can conduct with our children is to keep schooling the same at a time when every other aspect of our society is dramatically changing."*

It is even more relevant now as the pace of societal change and our knowledge base about how children learn and how to use assessment to improve learning has increased so dramatically over the intervening 25 plus years while so many aspects of "schooling," especially grading, have remained the same, allowing parents some comfort as school for their children was little different than when they were in school. This was mostly the case for grading and reporting with report cards commonly providing only a letter or percentage grade for each subject and sometimes short comments like "Vivian is a pleasure to teach" or "Elliot needs to participate more in class."

In this century, however, we came to understand that traditional grading was broken because grades were almost always inaccurate and inconsistent and promoted compliance, completion, and competition rather than learning and engagement. As a result, many schools have transitioned to grading practices known by a somewhat confusing variety of names and acronyms such as standards-based grading (SBG), standards-referenced grading (SRG), competency-based grading (CBG), and proficiency-based grading (PBG). There are some differences between each of these, but the essentials are the same, namely

1. grades based on standards/learning goals, not assessment methods;
2. levels of proficiency, not points and percentages; and
3. grades for achievement only with behaviors/dispositions reported separately.

Although I'm generally hesitant to endorse new terminology, I think that Matt and Chad's labeling all of these variants as "21st-century grading practices" is helpful.

Clarity about purpose is critical in everything we do, so it is necessary to see the value of Matt and Chad's book in terms of their stated purpose—*"to assist parents and guardians in understanding what is involved in 21st-century grading and assessment"* (xiv). And it is of great value because they definitely provide the philosophical underpinnings and practical examples to meet their purpose.

Every chapter starts with a scenario; sometimes as readers we skim these scenarios because we want to get into the main ideas, but you should pay attention to all of them because they very effectively set the scene for the issues discussed in each chapter. I particularly like the Jones family scenario in Chapter 1 and the divorced father's appreciation of his daughter's ownership of her learning in Chapter 5. Don't miss them!

Each chapter concludes with helpful questions for parents to ask students and teachers. It is my experience that the "hot button" issues, the issues that have the greatest misperceptions and create the most heated arguments, are often the same for parents trying to understand current practices as they are for educators resistant to the changes involved in 21st-century grading practices. Matt and Chad effectively address all these issues——hodgepodge grading, accountability/late submission of assessment evidence, college admission, electronic gradebooks/parent portals, homework/practice, reassessment, zeros, and what counts and why—with clarity and empathy for parents—and educators.

Matt and Chad "challenge parents amidst the wash of information, deadlines, and expectations to see the big picture," and that big picture is preparing students for their future, not their parents' or teachers' past. For quite a long time, I have seen that one of the huge benefits of 21st-century grading is that no longer is school just about achieving a high GPA that gets students into college but it is about preparing students to be successful in whatever they do beyond high school. This grading system is about student learning and developing students as self-regulated learners. The skills students need to be successful in their futures are critical thinking, listening and communication skills, and people skills, not the memorization and ability to write moderately well that may have served their parents well.

Another important issue that I was very pleased to see Matt and Chad address is the use of the word "work" in describing what students do and what they submit for evaluation by teachers. Some of my professional friends think that I have been obsessed by this, but I believe that we set a very different climate in our classrooms if we eliminate the word "work" and talk about students engaging in "learning activities" and providing "evidence of learning."

I never cease to be amazed by how prolific Matt Townsley is with writing articles and books about grading and reporting and by how many people he collaborates with in his writing. We have benefited from Matt and Chad's collaboration in the past, but this book is an even more valuable contribution because it fills a huge hole in the literature on grading by educating parents about 21st-century grading in ways that will enhance communication between schools and parents and with students and teachers. The book has the added value of supporting schools that have changed to 21st-century grading practices by providing parents with a practical and supportive guide. I'm very grateful to Matt and Chad for their excellent book and I'm confident that every parent and educator who reads the book will also be grateful.

Ken O'Connor
Toronto, ON, CANADA
December 2022

Acknowledgments

We would like to thank A. G. Wilson, Marty Williams, Ann Hoffman, Molly Fitch, Kerry Frank, Christian Gradgenett, Diane Townsley, David DenHartog, Ed Pavelec, and Tim Corcoran for their parent-perspective feedback on the contents of this book.

Thanks to Ken O'Connor for writing pioneering work in grading reform and for contributing the foreword for this book.

We would also like to thank our families for always being supportive of this project and the time and dedication it required.

Introduction

In the last century, few elements of the K–12 school experience have changed less than the role of grading. Twenty-first-century schools have evolved to meet the needs of what society has demanded students need to know and do, from reading, writing, and arithmetic to robotics, coding, advanced mathematics, and vocational education. More students attend school, graduate high school, and transition to post-secondary opportunities than ever before, but for all the K–12 educational reform, grading has remained relatively untouched in both premise and product (Brookhart et al., 2016). The United States has more tradition and emotion bound to the concept of grading than most any other nation in the world (Guskey, 2015). The concept of grades, their meaning, and implications are largely accepted by adults today, and understandably so, as many grades have serious consequences for a student's future path in both occupation and earnings.

Many schools have transitioned to grading practices such as *standards-based grading (SBG), standards-referenced grading (SRG), standards-based learning (SBL), competency-based grading, mastery grading, proficiency-based grading*, and even *ungrading*. We reference these efforts in this book as *21st-century grading practices*. While the specifics of these grading practices may differ from school to school, each of them intends to articulate a student's current level of learning more clearly in the gradebook or report card. Attempting to adopt a specific term is, in-and-of-itself, exclusionary and thus creates a feeling for parents, students, and schools of what grading *should* or *should not* be; therefore, we have elected to use a single umbrella term, *21st-century grading*. Our aim is to explore how 21st-century grading principles prepare students to thrive and grow based on feedback and communication of defined learning goals compared to traditional grading practices. Along the way, we provide readers with discussion questions to deepen their understanding in the local context.

WE WROTE THIS BOOK WITH PARENTS IN MIND

You may be picking up this book with a sense of curiosity about grades. Perhaps your children are attending schools utilizing grading practices that are unfamiliar to you. The gradebook or report card may not include letter grades, points, or even percentages and so you're left wondering, "How is my child doing?" and "Why do gradebooks and report cards look so different compared to when I was in school?"

In short, a century of research supports the idea that while grades may have been prevalent in American schools, reliability and validity of learning may not have (Brookhart et al., 2016; Finkelstein, 1913; Schinske & Tanner, 2014; Starch & Elliott, 1912). In fact, grades have become so convoluted and intertwined with compliance, ranking, sorting, and learning that a student, parent, or educator can often not tell you what a specific grade really means. Furthermore, the unparalleled educational fallout from the COVID-19 pandemic challenged schools, educators, and parents to assess the learning of students in new and innovative ways where traditional grading simply did not "make the grade." In hybrid or digital learning environments teachers and students found they could exchange demonstrations of learning without grade grubbing or point chasing. Some of the nation's largest school systems, such as Los Angeles Unified and San Diego Unified School Districts, implemented more transparent grading and assessment measures to better meet the needs of their students and improve in equitable grading practices (Esquivel, 2021). We should also note that some schools have implemented similar practices in years prior, while many more still cling to the outdated grading traditions of 20th century schools (Guskey et al., 2020; Townsley et al., 2019).

This book is designed for parents and schools alike, yet specifically oriented towards supporting parents in enhancing the clarity of communication of student learning between school and home. We know as both researchers and practitioners that change involving student grading can challenge some of the most common and widespread beliefs about how and what traditional grading practices have done for students over the last century of American education. While many schools have evolved in recent decades towards 21st-century grading practices, others are still mired in miscommunication, inaccuracy, and confusion associated with traditional grading practices. We believe that educating parents regarding the rationale behind transitioning to 21st-century grading practices is perhaps one of the most critical steps in solidifying the communication of student, school, and parent.

Few resources have been published in the past two decades aiming to support parents in furthering their understanding of 21st-century grading practices while also providing practical guiding questions to support better communication with their children and school alike. Solidifying home-school communication has been positively associated with improved student achievement outcomes, better attendance, and positive attitudes toward learning; outcomes all educators and parents can support (Lahey, 2019)!

Parents of 21st-century K–12 students can, understandably, struggle to keep pace with change in schools today; especially in comparison to many of their own school experiences. Technology integration, social pressures, college and career readiness expectations, and extracurricular opportunities provide for a vastly different educational experience. It can be overwhelming and leave parents feeling out-of-the loop and unknowledgable of how to support one's own children. This book unpacks the perils of traditional grading and articulates the tenets of 21st-century grading practices to provide a more common understanding for parents and educators today. Our chapters combine research on grading and assessment (you may notice our research references noted using parentheses) with practical scenarios and communication recommendations based on our experience as teachers and school leaders. We hope that parents will feel empowered to have more meaningful and purposeful communication about their child's learning with both their child and their child's educators. Moreover, we hope to improve the conversation for both parents and educators about prioritizing student *learning* over student *earning*. Understanding the purpose of 21st-century grading practices will reduce the likelihood of grades being bargained for as tokens of compliance. It is our hope this book will aid in reducing an "us versus them" mentality for students and parents while clarifying a system of grading that accurately represents what a child can know or do.

The purpose of this book is to assist parents and guardians in understanding what is involved in 21st-century grading and assessment. We believe this will enable parents and guardians to become better partners with educators in efforts to understand students' strengths and areas for improvement. Specifically, this book is designed to help parents and guardians:

1. understand how education has changed since they were in school,
2. recognize the limits of information typically communicated through electronic gradebooks and report cards,
3. appreciate the information communicated through standards-based gradebooks and report cards, and
4. identify how 21st-century grading and assessment benefits their student(s).

Based upon informal conversations with parents, empirical research, and our personal experiences, this book also aims to support schools that have changed their grading practices by providing a practical and supportive guide specifically written for parents.

HOW THIS BOOK IS ORGANIZED

Our book is organized in a purposeful way to help parents first understand the rationale for 21st-century grading practices. Next, we explain the implications of these grading practices and how they benefit students. Finally, we help readers understand how to best partner with educators in schools implementing 21st-century grading practices.

Rationale

In the first chapter, we describe why school gradebooks and/or report cards look different than when many parents were in school. Through an enhanced understanding of the changing landscape of education and the perils of electronic gradebook *scoreboard watching*, readers will begin to understand standards-based gradebooks and report cards.

In the second chapter, we describe *why* schools are changing their grading practices. Twenty-first-century careers value both employability skills and academic competency; therefore, some schools are choosing to report them separately in the gradebook or report card.

Implications

The third chapter details how these 21st-century grading practices address student accountability. In doing so, implications for the real world and the fallacy of motivation are also considered.

The fourth chapter is written for parents of high school or soon-to-be high school students. When schools use 21st-century grading practices, specific questions often arise related to grade point averages, scholarships, and post-high-school positioning. Getting *into* college and getting *through* college are both important topics discussed in this chapter.

Partnering

Finally, Chapter 5 invites parents to partner with educators in the grading and feedback process. When 21st-century grading practices are in place, parents should know more precisely what is being expected of their child. To ensure the book is practical for readers, each chapter ends with a series of questions for parents to ask their students and their students' teachers.

The following chapters will not answer all parent questions related to grading; however, they will offer a more thorough understanding of 21st-century grading practices and provide helpful questions to ask children and children's teachers to ensure there is common understanding of what the gradebook or report card communicates about the learner. This book is not intended to scrutinize individual teachers' or schools' grading practices. Within our umbrella term of "21st-century grading practices," there is considerable room for variation and context, yet the aim remains the same: communicating students' current strengths and areas for improvement relative to defined learning goals.

End-of-Chapter Reflective Questions

Because this book is written in efforts to maximize the clarity and effectiveness of the parent–school dialogue, we have included a feature at the end of each chapter, "Opportunities to Continue the Conversation." These are reflective questions for parents and guardians to consider in supporting communication of *learning* over *earning* for their children and with their respective teachers. These questions are meant to stimulate growth-minded conversations with children and encourage them to take ownership of their learning journey. They are not intended to be used verbatim, but rather as starting points or question stems that parents can adapt to their own school and context. The reflection stems for teachers are designed to help parents ask supportive questions of their child's educators. Overall, the benefits of "being on the same page" produce a supportive learning environment necessary for optimal student development and academic achievement while providing clarity of feedback for strengths and weaknesses needed for future success.

Chapter 1

Help!

Why Does My Child's Gradebook and Report Card Look Different than When I Was In School?

Consider the following conversation between parents and their 5th-grade student when examining a school report card.

> Cassy and Nathan Jones are at the kitchen table discussing their child's first-quarter report card. With parent-teacher conferences coming up next week with 5th-grade Mrs. Johnson, this middle-class couple is attempting to understand the annotations on their oldest son's report card. Caleb is a 5th-grade student and his school's new report card includes a series of statements such as "Reads and writes decimals to thousandths" and "Adds, subtracts, multiplies, and divides decimals using a variety of strategies." While these math statements sound familiar to Nathan's parents, the additional notes next to each statement create some confusion.
>
> Cassy Jones wonders, "What does it mean for my son to be '*developing*' in reading and writing decimals? Is this like a C or a D?" Nathan chimes in sarcastically, "I think it means Nathan only has seven tenths of the decimals figured out." Caleb yells from the room next door, "Dad! That's not what it means. '*Developing*' means that Mrs. Johnson says I still have some work to do with decimals." Cassy Jones laments the "good old days" when she received As, Bs, and Cs on *her* 5th-grade report card many years ago, and how those letter grades were based upon percentages. In talking with some of the other area moms, they have attributed this change at the school to "standards-based grading."
>
> She has been told that 5th-grade parents can now track their child's current progress on each standard using a smartphone app. She previously downloaded the app but was confused when she did not see any numbers or percentages, so she removed it from her phone after a few days. Suddenly, Nathan Jones grabs the report card out of his wife's hands and begins to read it. In doing so, he wonders to himself, "What in the world does '*beginning*' mean for Caleb next to 'Uses punctuation to separate items in a series.' Does this mean my son is failing commas and semicolons?"

The Jones family scenario is all too common for households experiencing changes in their school's grading and reporting practices. As noted in the Introduction, many schools have transitioned to 21st-century grading practices, which encompass *standards-based grading* (SBG), *standards-referenced grading* (SRG), *competency-based grading*, *mastery grading*, and even *ungrading*. The overall intent of 21st-century grading practices is to articulate a student's current level of learning more clearly in the gradebook or report card. While some of the nation's largest school systems, such as Los Angeles Unified and San Diego Unified School Districts, have implemented more transparent grading and assessment measures to better meet the needs of their students and improve in equitable grading practices, were in response to lessons learned from COVID-19 (Esquivel, 2021; Taketa, 2020), some smaller school districts were implementing similar practices in previous years (Buckmiller et al., 2020; Knight & Cooper, 2019; Townsley, 2013; Townsley et al., 2019). Regardless of a school's current grading practices, the COVID-19 pandemic caused a growing number of schools to reconsider the way students *could* and *should* be graded (Guskey, 2021; Townsley, 2021).

In this chapter we will:

- Provide a brief overview of the changing landscape of education leading up to COVID-19 in order to better understand the purpose of grades.
- Discuss the perils of electronic gradebook and "scoreboard watching" in the modern era.
- Offer an in-depth rationale for standards-based gradebooks and report cards, which includes several visual examples.
- Provide opportunities at the end of this chapter for you to continue the conversation with your child and your child's educators.

A HISTORICAL LOOK AT THE CHANGING LANDSCAPE OF EDUCATION

The No Child Left Behind Act of 2001 was bipartisan legislation spearheaded by President George W. Bush that applied to all K–12 public schools in the United States (U.S. Department of Education, 2004). This legislation is commonly referred to as NCLB and dramatically changed the landscape of education. Prior to NCLB, the previous major federal reform movement, the Elementary and Secondary Education Act (ESEA), did not hold public schools accountable based upon student achievement.

The intent of NCLB was to provide more equitable opportunities for *all* students in public education (Klein, 2015). In particular, NCLB aimed to make schools accountable for traditionally underrepresented subgroups of students, such as students in poverty, minority students, students receiving special education services, and students who speak limited English (Klein, 2015). Accountability took place through required annual testing and reporting of the test results. Under NCLB, states were initially required to develop and administer tests for students in math and reading in grades 3 through 8 and at least once in high school. Several years later, states were also required to test students in science at least once in grades 3 through 5, at least once in grades 6 through 9, and at least once in grades 10 through 12. Using increasingly stringent and moving goalposts over time, NCLB set a target that required *all* students to reach proficiency by 2014 (Kim & Sunderman, 2005). These accountability measures often placed an increased emphasis on preparing students for the test (Rush & Scherff, 2012). For arguably the first time in the history of public education, *what* students learned in math, reading, and science was being measured in a standardized way across an entire state.

When any single subgroup did not meet the targets established by NCLB in consecutive years, a school was labeled as "in need of improvement" (Simpson et al., 2004). In addition to labels, schools may also have been sanctioned by the state department of education. For example, schools were required to notify parents when their school received a subpar rating, and if the sanctions continued, parents were required to be offered the option of transferring their child to a higher performing school (Howell, 2006). In order to ensure teachers were effective in helping students learn based upon these standardized measures, other schools who did not meet the targets over multiple years may have been required to fire all of their staff members and invite them all to re-apply for their jobs, or to reorganize the entire school (Mitani, 2018).

The standardized tests used for reporting and accountability were often established on a state-by-state basis. For example, the state test for Iowa students was called the Iowa Assessments, and the state test for students in California was the California Standards Test. Some consortiums of states utilize common assessments, such as the Smarter Balanced Assessments Consortium (n.d.). Most often, these standardized state tests included predominantly multiple-choice questions (Darling-Hammond, 2007) that were efficient, and therefore, cost effective to score. In Figure 1.1 below, you will see a math question that is similar to what 6th-grade students would see as a part of the New York State Testing Program. This question, and many questions on this exam, are multiple-choice, which allows them to be quickly scored. In addition, these multiple-choice questions assess students' learning that is limited to little, or no actual context, in a rote manner which emphasizes memorization.

Prior to NCLB, the expectation for what K–12 students learned was a local rather than state decision and as such, what students learned often varied from school to school. Due to this inconsistency, the math concepts students learned in one 3rd-grade classroom could have been significantly different between counties or school districts. During the NCLB era each state was required to annually administer tests in the areas of math, reading, and science, often for the first time; therefore, each state established a common set of learning expectations for students in these three content areas. These common sets of learning expectations are commonly referred to as the "state standards." Using these statewide standards, every 3rd-grade student, for example, would be learning the same math concepts across the state, with an emphasis on preparation for the state math standardized test.

In 2009, a group of 48 state leaders, including governors and state commissioners of education, launched an effort to create a list of standards that students would be expected to learn, regardless of the state where their school is located (CCSS, n.d.). In this attempt to create a set of standards that would help students become "college and career ready," and with the input of state education leaders and classroom teachers, the Common Core State Standards were released in June 2010. This initial version of the Common Core State Standards included common expectations for K–12 students in reading, writing, and math. Yet, merely establishing these standards did not mean all states were requiring them. As of 2022, 41 states, Washington, DC, and four U.S. territories had voluntarily adopted the Common Core State Standards (Common Core State Standards, n.d.).

Although NCLB was initially a bipartisan effort, implementing this one-size-fits-all federal legislation eventually brought with it plenty of criticism. Some critics believed NCLB was an underfunded mandate in that it required schools to make significant changes to the textbooks and other classroom supplies needed to teach the state standards and adequately prepare

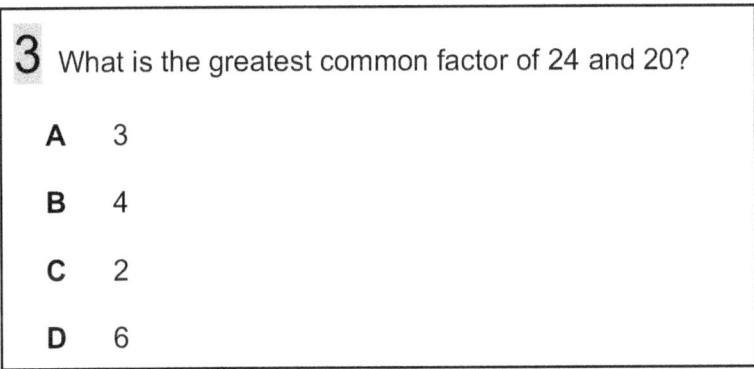

Figure 1.1 Sample question from a 6th-grade New York standardized test

students for the state standardized test (Dee et al., 2013). In particular, urban schools were faced with budget constraints that did not allow them to attract and retain quality teachers needed to educate an often transient and perhaps more challenging student population (Dee et al., 2013). Other critics strongly suggested that NCLB placed too much emphasis on using standardized tests to measure student achievement (Darling-Hammond, 2014; Hursh, 2007). When faced with increased pressure to teach to the test, teachers may not have time to teach concepts not easily tested using multiple choice questions or those in content areas not on the test. For example, social studies teachers reported having less time during the school day to dedicate to their subject area, which NCLB did not require to be assessed (Winstead, 2011).

After several years of failed attempts to reform education at the federal level, in 2015, NCLB was replaced by the Every Student Succeeds Act (commonly referred to as ESSA). ESSA (n.d.) affects every student in K–12 public schools across the United States. Rather than requiring common learning accountability metrics for all states, ESSA (n.d.) permitted individual states to create their own plan within parameters established by the federal government. These parameters included incorporating "challenging" academic learning standards, annual testing, school accountability, goals for student achievement, plans for supporting struggling schools, and publishing statewide information about how each school is performing. Because NCLB critics believed too much emphasis was being placed on standardized tests and communicating only these results, ESSA permitted states to develop unique plans in which schools are rated based upon test scores as well as additional factors, such as graduation rates (Portz & Beauchamp, 2022).

Labels are no longer mandated for the lowest performing schools. Yet school performance metrics, however each state defines them, are still required to be published for public consumption (Council of Chief State School Officers, 2022). See Figures 1.2a, 1.2b, 1.2c, and 1.2d below for a four-page excerpt from an Arizona state report on Santa Rosa Elementary School's performance.

Santa Rosa Elementary School
Maricopa Unified School District

2022

School Details

Overview

Grades Served ①
Preschool - Grade 6

District
Maricopa Unified School District

Principal
N/A

Mission Statement
N/A

School Type
District School

Title I Status ②
Yes

School Grade
Ⓐ

Location

21400 N SANTA ROSA DR, MARICOPA, AZ, 85138-4215

Contact

(520) 568-6150

① Please review the data below to get more details on the grade levels a school serves. Some Arizona high schools offer specialty programs such as a Career and Technical Education Early Education classes (preschool) or advanced mathematics courses for junior high students. These students' actual grade levels will be reflected in their "grades served" and are not levels that exist in whole at the school site.

② A Title I school is a school receiving federal funds for Title I students. The basic principle of Title I is that schools with large concentrations of low-income students will receive supplemental funds to assist in meeting students educational goals. All other schools are Non-Title I.

Figure 1.2a. Excerpt of a school performance profile for Santa Rosa Elementary School

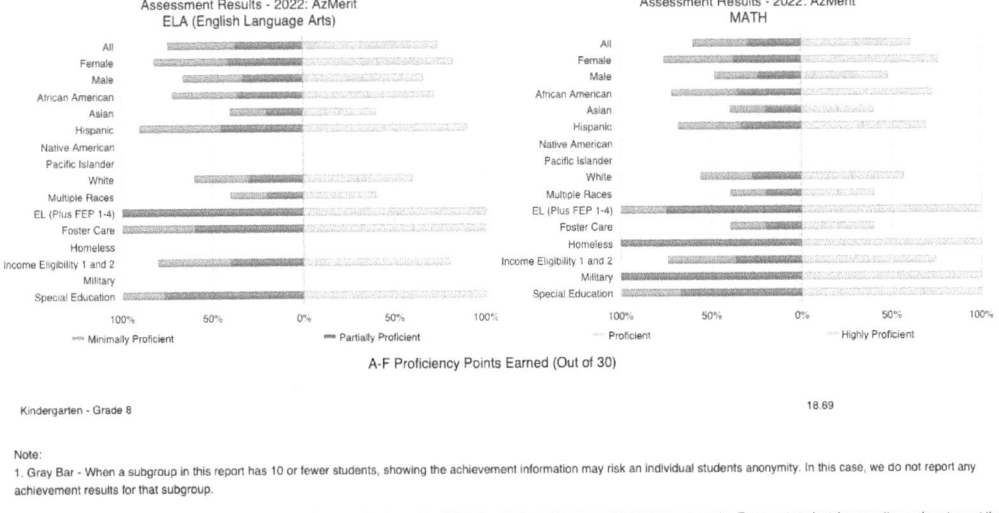

Figure 1.2b. Excerpt of a school performance profile for Santa Rosa Elementary School

ESSA requires states to assess students annually in reading/writing and math in grades 3 through 8 as well as once in high school, and once in science in elementary school, once in middle school, and once in high school. These assessments are developed based upon the state's standards in math, reading/writing, and science. Like NCLB, the results of these assessments for *all* tested students as well as subgroups, such as students living in poverty and minority students, and English Language Learners, are required to be reported according to ESSA.

STANDARDS-BASED GRADEBOOKS AND REPORT CARDS

While ESSA requires each *state* and *school district* to report how they're doing on an annual basis, many parents are interested in knowing how *their child* is doing, and on a more frequent basis. As schools are held increasingly accountable for student learning as measured by standardized tests that are aligned with state standards, more schools are making the shift to standards-based gradebooks and report cards. Prior to NCLB and ESSA, not many states had required state standards.

When comparing 21st-century grading practices, there are subtle differences; however, all of these grading practices involve the use of gradebooks that focus on communicating some granularity of the state's standards. For example, when schools utilize standards-based gradebooks and/or standards-based report cards, they are based upon these required state *standards*. A school using a target-based grading system may utilize finer-grained descriptions of these state standards, which are called *targets*. Similarly, schools using language such as competencies encompass broader statements that align with multiple state standards. For the purpose of this book, when we refer to standards-based gradebooks, we are referring to all gradebooks that are based upon standards, targets, or competencies.

Growth Performance

The school was included in the A-F State Accountability model for growth by having enough qualifying data points. Growth is determined by how individual students perform compared to their previous scoring history and if they are on target to continuously improve or stay within the highest rankings of proficiency.

Growth Performance A-F Points Earned: 2023(Out of 50)

Kindergarten - Grade 8   48.88

End Of Year Promotion

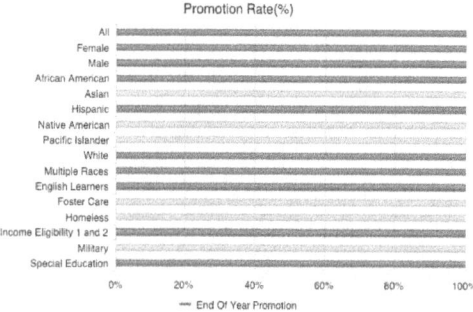

Note:
*When a subgroup in this report has 10 or fewer students, showing Promotion Rate may risk an individual student's anonymity. In this case, we do not report any information for that subgroup.

School Finance

Funding for Arizona public schools is driven primarily by student enrollment, generally increasing and decreasing with the number of students served, but many student-specific, district-specific, and charter-specific factors also affect funding. For example, students with certain special education needs generate more funding than students without special education needs. English Learners and students in specific grades also receive add-on funding. Small school districts and charter organizations are provided greater funding per student than their larger counterparts since smaller organizations lack the economies of scale enjoyed by larger organizations. Additionally, school districts can raise funds through local property taxes and can seek voter-approval to increase funding while charters, which do not have the ability to levy local property taxes, instead receive a higher per-pupil allocation from the state.

Spending for schools is directed by the district or charter governing board and will vary from school to school based on local needs and priorities. For example, if one school has more experienced teachers than another school, spending for teacher pay and benefits is likely to be higher at that site. A school in a rural district is likely to have higher spending for transportation than a school in a densely-populated area in which many students walk to school. A school that provides career and technical education or hosts a specialized program might have higher costs for supplies or other related areas as a result.

Revenue and expenditure data for Arizona public schools should be viewed within the context of schools' unique characteristics.

Please https://schoolspending.az.gov/explore/as-parent-guardian/school/110220104 to visit the Arizona School Financial Transparency Portal to view detailed school and district/charter level financial data

Per-Pupil Expenditures of Federal, State and Local Funds

Expenditures summarized by actual personnel expenditures and actual non-personnel expenditures (1) separate by source of funds or funds, Federal or State & Local, for each publicly funded Local Education Agency (LEA) - school and charter districts. Expenditures are divided by the aggregate number of students enrolled in preschool through Grade 12 in publicly funded LEAs on or around October 1 of a given year. Per-Pupil expenditures are supplementary categorized by Title I classification for schools within the district.

Per-Pupil Expenditure: 2022

Personnel Federal Expenditure	Personnel State & Local Expenditure	Non-Personnel Federal Expenditure	Non-Personnel State & Local Expenditure	Total Per-Pupil Expenditure
$ 597.84	$ 9,364.69	$ 1,011.22	$ 1,089.85	$ 12,063.61

1. Excluded are expenditures for land and improvements, buildings, and improvements, furniture, equipment and vehicles. Also excluded are Internal Service Fund operations. Community School Fund operations, debt retirement, student activities and non-public school programs.

Disclaimer:
Expenditure data is compiled from unaudited information submitted to the Arizona Department of Education.

Per-Pupil Characteristics

Personnel	Non-Personnel
No data available	No data available

Figure 1.2c. Excerpt of a school performance profile for Santa Rosa Elementary School

Acceleration Readiness

Kindergarten - Grade 8 Acceleration Readiness is calculated from different components: Subgroup Improvement in Math and English Language arts, reducing the percent of 3rd graders in the Minimally Proficient category on the state English Language Arts Assessment, improving chronic absenteeism and Special Education Inclusion.

Acceleration Readiness A-F Points Earned: 2023 (Out of 10)

Acceleration Readiness A-F Points	10

State Accountability A-F Letter Grades

Arizona Revised Statutes § 15-241 requires the Arizona Department of Education, subject to final adoption by the State Board of Education, to develop an annual achievement profile for every public school in the state based on an A through F scale.

The system measures year to year student academic growth, proficiency on English language arts, math and science. It also includes the proficiency and academic growth of English language learners, indicators that an elementary student is ready for success in high school and that high school students are ready to succeed in a career or higher education and high school graduation rates. For more information on State Accountability, https://azreportcards.azed.gov/static/A-FSummaryFY19 .

A-F Summary: 2022

K-8 Model

	K-8 Points Earned	K-8 Points Eligible
Proficiency	18.69	30
Growth	48.88	50
EL Growth and Proficiency	10	10
Acceleration Readiness	10	10
Bonus Points*	3.5	5**
Total Points	87.57	
Percentage	91.07	

K-8 Model Cut Scores

A	B	C	D	F
84.67 - 100%	72.39 - 84.66%	60.11 - 72.38%	47.83 - 60.10%	< 47.82%

Letter Grade: A

Schools receiving a NR (Not-Rated) currently do not have the components required in the current model to receive a grade.

**Up to 5 extra bonus points can be earned by K-8 schools. Bonus points are added to the final percentage earned.

*K-8 Bonus points can be earned in the following ways: Special Education enrollment greater than or equal to 80% of the state average, high performance on the state Science assessment.

Figure 1.2d. Excerpt of a school performance profile for Santa Rosa Elementary School

Standards-Based Gradebooks

Standards-based gradebooks communicate a child's level of learning using state standards. Standards-based gradebooks differ from traditional gradebooks in that they communicate current competency of a standard rather than accumulation of points by a category or weight (such as tests and homework). While a test may traditionally be worth 50 points, this same test is now entered into the gradebook using a more granular level of communication. Today, resulting from these federal testing requirements, nearly every state has required content standards.

For example, if the Biology Unit 8 test assessed a child's learning of two science standards, then these two science standards would be noted in the electronic gradebook. Similar to how a multi-point inspection from a mechanic provides a detailed assessment of a vehicle, a standards-based gradebook provides a more detailed perspective on a child's current levels of learning based upon the standards. See Table 1.1 for an example of standards-based gradebook for a science class. The standards students were expected to learn include *Newton's 3rd law*, *representing models for waves*, and *developing models for waves*.

Table 1.1. Sample standards-based gradebook for an 8th-Grade science student

Date	Standard	Current Level of Learning
September 12	Apply Newton's 3rd law (MS-PS2–1)	*Proficient*
October 1	Use mathematical representations to describe a model for waves that includes how amplitude is related to energy (MS-PS4–1)	*Developing*
October 16	Develop and use a model to describe that waves are reflected, absorbed, or transmitted through various materials (MS-PS4–2)	*Proficient*

The student in Table 1.1 is doing very well at demonstrating Newton's 3rd Law (*Proficient* on September 12) and developing a model to describe waves (*Proficient* on October 16); however, additional learning needs to be demonstrated for this student in using mathematical representations to describe a model for waves (*Developing* on October 1). This sample standards-based gradebook provides a detailed perspective on the 8th-grade child's current levels of learning as of October 16.

It should also be noted that entries in electronic standards-based gradebooks, while digital, are not necessarily permanent until the end of the reporting period (e.g. quarter, trimester, or semester). This shift in viewing gradebooks as dynamic, rather than static, within 21st-century grading practices will be detailed further in Chapter 3.

Some schools, in particular high schools, choose to determine a letter grade based upon a child's current level of learning for the standards in the subject or course. When a letter grade is determined at the end of a reporting period (e.g., quarter, trimester, or semester), this iteration of 21st-century grading practices provides students and parents with the specific areas of strength and growth within the gradebook itself. It also may aid future employers or college admissions personnel in making informed decisions by providing familiar information, including grades and grade point averages (GPAs), on high school transcripts. In this book, we do not dive into the specifics of how letter grades are determined based on standards in the gradebook at the end of a reporting period. However, if this aspect of 21st-century grading practices is being implemented in your child's school, we recommend that you contact the school to learn more about the determination process. Understanding how grades are assigned can help you better understand your child's progress and support their learning. It is understandable that parents may be concerned about changes to grading practices and the potential consequences or implications of the higher education admissions process. Yet, research has indicated this is not the case, which we discuss further in Chapter 4.

Standards-Based Report Cards

Other schools using 21st-century grading practices may choose to not determine a letter grade at all for each subject or course. Instead, the child's current level of learning is communicated on a *standards-based report card*. As a parent reading this book, you may be familiar with the format of *your* report card as an elementary student. These report cards included marks such as S for *satisfactory* and a check mark for *needs further improvement*. The indicators on these elementary report cards from years ago were locally determined. That is, if your 3rd-grade teacher noted your *satisfactory* level of learning for multiplication facts, this did not necessarily mean that *all* 3rd-grade students in your school systems, and certainly not all 3rd-grade students across the entire state, were necessarily being taught multiplication facts in this grade.

Today, standards-based report cards do not include a letter grade on the report card and instead communicate a child's level of learning for a variety of school-selected standards from

| | David Douglas School District 40 | | | Report Card |
| | Portland, Oregon | | | Grade 1 |

Student Information
Student Name:	
Student ID:	
School Year:	
Grade:	1
Teacher:	

School Information
School Name:	
Principal:	
School Phone:	
School Address:	

Attendance	Semester 1	Semester 2
Days Present		
Days Absent		
Attendance Rate		
Tardy or Left Early		

Student Services
Active ELL	
Monitored ELL	
Talented and Gifted	
Special Education	

Proficiency Scale
4	Proficient	The student consistently demonstrates mastery of the grade level standards. Evidence shows ability to apply concepts in a variety of contexts.
3	Approaching Proficiency	The student is able to demonstrate partial understanding of the grade level standards. Student still produces evidence that may often contain errors.
2	Minimal Proficiency	The student is not demonstrating understanding of the grade level standards. Student produces evidence that is significantly below grade level.
1	Insufficient Evidence Towards Proficiency	There is a lack of evidence to determine proficiency of the grade level standards.
NA	Not Applicable	The standard was not addressed this semester or the student was not enrolled long enough to accurately assess.

READING	S1	S2
Demonstrate understanding of spoken words, syllables, and sounds. RF.2		
Know spelling and sounds for common digraphs (e.g. sh, th, ph). RF.3a		
Know "final e" (e.g. made) and vowel teams to represent vowel sounds (e.g. boat, eat). RF.3c		
Read words with inflectional endings correctly (e.g. -s, -ed, -ing). RF.3f		
Read grade-appropriate irregularly spelled words. RF.3g		
Read grade level text with accuracy and fluency to support comprehension. RF.4, RF.1		
Ask and answer questions about key details in a text (fiction and non-fiction). RL.1, RL.4, SL.2		
Retell stories with key details and identify the message of the story. RL.2, RL.6, RL.9, RI.8		
Describe characters, settings, and major events in a story. RL.3, RL.7		
Explain major differences between books that tell stories and books that give information. RL.5, RI.3, RI.9		
Identify the main topic and retell key details of a text. RI.2, RI.1, RI.7		
Know and use various text features (e.g. Headings, Tables of Contents, Diagrams, Labels, Glossaries) to locate key facts or information in a text. RI.5, RI.6		
With prompting and support, read grade level text. RI.10, RL.10, RI.4		

WRITING	S1	S2
Write an opinion piece with an introduction, opinion, supporting reason and conclusion. W.1		
Write an informative paper with a topic, facts, and an ending sentence. W.2		
Write a narrative story with events placed in the correct order and provide a sense of closure. W.3, W.6, SL.5		
With guidance and support from adults, focus on a topic, respond to questions and suggestions from peers, and add details to strengthen writing. W.5		
Work with others to write about a research topic. W.7, W.8		
Demonstrate command of capitalization, punctuation, and spelling when writing (e.g., capitalize dates and names of people, spell new words phonetically and use known spelling rules, etc.). L.2		

Figure 1.3a. First-grade standards-based report card from David Douglas School District in Portland, Oregon. *Reprinted with permission of David Douglas School District in Portland, Oregon (2023)*

the list of state standards. The number of standards on the report card will likely vary from content area to content area. To save space, the standards included on report cards often represent a selection of the full set of academic standards required by the state. See Figures 1.3a, 1.3b, 1.3c for a three-page example of a 1st-grade standards-based report card.

In this three-page report card, there are standards listed for each content area: 13 in reading, 6 in writing, 3 in language, 2 in speaking and listening, 15 in mathematics, 3 in science,

Student:	Grade: 1	Teacher:		

LANGUAGE	S1	S2
Demonstrate command of the conventions of standard english grammar and usage when writing or speaking (e.g., use of nouns, verbs, adjectives, pronouns, prepositions, conjunctions, etc.) **L.1**		
Determine the meaning of unknown and multiple meaning words and phrases by using context clues, prefixes, suffixes and root words. **L.4**, L.5		
Use new words and phrases when speaking, reading, and writing. **L.6**		

SPEAKING AND LISTENING	S1	S2
Participate in small and large group conversations, follow agreed upon rules for discussion, build on others' ideas, and ask questions to clear up confusion. **SL.1**, SL.3		
Using details produce complete sentences to express ideas and feelings clearly. **SL.6**, SL.4		

MATHEMATICS	S1	S2
Model and solve addition and subtraction word problems using objects, drawings and equations with unknown numbers in different positions. **OA.1**, OA.2		
Show that changing the order of the numbers does not change the answer (e.g. 2+3+1=5+1=6 or 8+3=11 is the same as 3+8=11). **OA.3**		
Add and subtract within 20, using known strategies. **OA.6**, OA.5		
Demonstrate fluency for addition and subtraction within 10. **OA.6**		
Understand the meaning of the equal sign, and determine if the equations involving addition and subtraction are true or false (e.g. 4+3=5+2). **OA.7**		
Determine the unknown whole number in an addition or subtraction equation when two out of the three numbers are given (8+?=11, 5=?-3, 6+6=?). **OA.8**, OA.4		
Count to 120, starting at any number less than 120. Read and write any number up to 120, represent the number of objects with the written number. **NBT.1**		
Determine when and explain why a two digit number is greater than, less than, or equal to another two digit number, record the comparison using the symbols >, < and =. **NBT.3**, NBT.2, NBT.5		
Use concrete models or drawings to add within 100, without regrouping. **NBT.4**		
Subtract a mulitple of 10 from a multiple of 10, using concrete models or drawings and strategies based on place value. (e.g. 80-20, 50-30) **NBT.6**		
Order three objects by length; compare the lengths of two objects indirectly by using a third object. **MD.1**, MD.2		
Tell and write time in hours and half-hours using analog and digital clocks. **MD.3**		
Organize, represent, and interpret data with up to three categories. **MD.4**		
Create new shapes using two-dimensional and three-dimensional shapes. **G.2**, G.1		
Describe the equal parts of a circle and rectangle with words (halves, fourths, and quarters). **G.3**		

SCIENCE	S1	S2
Life Science: Understand parts of animals/plants are similar and different, helping them survive and grow. **1-LS1**, **1-LS3**, **K-2-ETS1**		
Waves: Understand sound and light are types of waves that can interact with objects differently. **1-PS4**		
Space Systems: Understand the sun, moon, and stars demonstrate patterns and cycles. **1-ESS1**		

SOCIAL SCIENCE	S1	S2
Understand the concepts of units taught (Civics/Government, Economics, History, and Geography).		

HEALTH	S1	S2
Understand the concepts of units taught.		

PHYSICAL EDUCATION	S1	S2
Be actively engaged and participate.		
Demonstrate competency in motor skills and movement patterns.		

MUSIC EDUCATION	S1	S2
Sing with appropriate range and tone.		
Perform on instruments with appropriate technique.		
Interpret and apply musical notation, vocabulary, and symbols.		

Figure 1.3b. First-grade standards-based report card from David Douglas School District in Portland, Oregon

Student:	Grade: 1		Teacher:		
SUCCESS SKILLS (Unmarked spaces show areas of student success / X indicates student needs improvement)					
	S1	S2		S1	S2
Works independently and manages time effectively			Demonstrates respect for adults, students, school environment, and materials		
Actively participates in learning			Makes appropriate transitions between activities		
Produces quality work			Organizes self, materials, and belongings		
Listens attentively and follows directions			Uses problem solving skills		
Takes responsibility for choices and actions			Completes assignments on time		
Follows school routines and expectations					

TEACHER COMMENTS

Semester 1

Semester 2

David Douglas School District
Portland, Oregon
Learn · Grow · Thrive

Figure 1.3c. First-grade standards-based report card from David Douglas School District in Portland, Oregon

1 in social sciences, 1 in health, 2 in physical education, 3 in music education, and 11 success skills. Academic standards (i.e., "Reading") are reported separately from non-academic standards (i.e., "Success Skills"). Each student's level of learning for each standard during a report period at David Douglas School District in Portland, Oregon, is noted with a 4 for *proficient,* 3 for *approaching proficiency*, 2 for *minimal proficiency*, 1 for *insufficient evidence towards proficiency,* and "NA" for not applicable when a standard was not addressed in the semester, or the student was not enrolled long enough to accurately assess.

COMMUNICATING LEVELS OF LEARNING

Whether a school is using a standards-based gradebook or a standards-based report card, they will choose to use a consistent set of marks to indicate progress towards learning the standard. Some schools will choose to utilize numerals and corresponding descriptions of learning to indicate levels, as was the case with David Douglas School District. Other schools may use letters such as P for *proficient* and D for *developing*. The numbers and letters are qualitative rather than quantitative descriptors of learning. This means that a 4 does not represent twice as much as a 2 level of learning. Each level of learning, whether a number or letter, is often associated with a standard scale that defines the level of proficiency. Parents are encouraged to read and understand report card keys, if provided. Often, there are no percentages noted on standards-based report cards. For an in-depth description of percentage-based grading, see Chapter 3.

Twenty-First-Century Grading and the COVID-19 Pandemic

Standards-based gradebooks and report cards are not entirely new; yet due to the COVID-19 pandemic, more schools are considering alternative and standards-based grading practices (Guskey, 2021; Townsley, 2021). During this time of pandemic-induced remote learning, educators assigning points based upon assignments completed at home outside of school hours may not have accurately reflected what a student can and cannot do. Families with helpful resources such as reliable internet access, and parents who were more often home and able to assist their children with academic work, were at a significant advantage when compared to families without these resources. For additional discussion on the implications of assigning points for assignments completed at home, see Chapter 2.

As such, some schools established or considered policies to only include assignments completed *during* school hours when determining a student's final grade (Minock, 2021). Citing similar situations in which homelife might have been unpredictable, other schools established policies to permit students to turn in assignments late without penalty (Sawchuck, 2020). For example, Woodinville High School in the North Shore District in Woodinville, Washington (n.d.), permitted students to turn in assignments up to one week late without penalty during the pandemic school years. An examination of states' departments of education guidance during the Spring 2020 building closures suggests that schools were often provided these flexibility and equity considerations (Townsley & Kunnath, 2022). Many schools continue to honor such equitable practices as schools began to return to in-person learning post-pandemic, citing less stress and focus on "point grubbing" and more focus on learning.

The Perils of the Electronic Gradebook and "Scoreboard Watching"

Perhaps grades are more front and center to parents because of the ability to access them on demand through electronic gradebooks, but much like the stock market, the data is only as good as our ability to interpret it. We encourage utilizing digital means to stay up to date with a child's academic and behavioral progress, but not unless you have a full understanding of what the key indicators, markings, and scores mean and do not mean.

From a historical perspective, students and parents have not always had universal access to the gradebook. Teachers would often use a "big red book" to keep track of their students' assignment completion and assessment scores. Only the teacher was able to view this gradebook and there was no need to organize it in a way for others to interpret. Traditionally, grades were mailed home to families at the end of each quarter or semester. A gradebook, similar to a medical chart used by a family physician, contains a lot of personalized information and may include codes that are specific to the teacher or administrator. As parents view modern-day electronic gradebooks, we suggest that they inquire with teachers and/or with the school to better understand the setup and meaning of electronic gradebook information. Merely accessing information does not always equate to appropriately interpreting it!

Today, using a software application such as PowerSchool, Infinite Campus, or Skyward, many schools provide parents with electronic gradebook access to their child's academic information. The information available to parents has traditionally been communicated through tests, projects, papers, worksheets, or other assignments. Typically, these gradebooks have emphasized the modality of assessment (e.g., quiz or test) and communicated using points and percentages to parents rather than learning goals, and levels of proficiency. As such, we urge parents to ask more clarifying questions about what and how student grades are being computed. Grades are only as meaningful as the evidence entered into an electronic gradebook. Guskey (2002) found that electronic gradebooks have the appearance of being more objective and accurate, but there can be a big difference between precision and accuracy. A student's science grade of 89.22% appears to be highly precise, but it does not accurately communicate the extent to which a student has demonstrated understanding of the science learning goals and standards in the course.

You may be familiar with a common practice in elementary and some middle schools of sending home progress reports. These progress reports represent a snapshot of a student's learning at approximately the halfway point of a quarter, trimester, or other reporting period. While some schools have stopped sending home these progress reports due to the prevalent access of electronic gradebooks, others have continued this tradition. Parents should be aware of the fact that their *students' learning is continuing to progress* during the reporting period; therefore, these progress reports may not accurately reflect where a student will actually be at the *end of the reporting period*. Progress reports communicate a portion of the journey, and we suggest parents keep this in mind as they seek to monitor their student's progress.

In the initial scenario presented in this chapter, the Jones family experienced changes in their school's grading and reporting practices. Uncertainty surrounding the information being provided in the electronic gradebook created confusion within the family: Cassy and Nathan Jones were more familiar with traditional points-based communication in the gradebook. These well-intentioned parents were familiar with interpreting the information provided by the school through the gradebook, and now the flow of information was seemingly in a new format. The roots of this misunderstanding may come depending upon their personal experiences as K–12 students rather than a full understanding of 21st-century grading practices.

In the past, school personnel have strongly recommended that parents sign up for on-demand access to their child's electronic gradebook as well as for notifications via email or text message related to their child's grades. Options for receiving these communications often include daily, weekly, or immediately after an assignment's grade has been published. Similar to receiving just-in-time updates on news headlines and sports team scores, parents are able to "watch" their child's electronic gradebook with ease. Through what we refer to as "scoreboard watching," parents have just-in-time access to their child's electronic gradebook, which enables them to keep a close eye on any positive or negative changes in the gradebook. For example, if the Unit 5 test lands on a Friday, parents find themselves regularly waiting for the teacher to enter the score into the gradebook. While we applaud the efforts of parents who choose to receive regular updates on their child's progress, we believe this practice emphasizes the importance of *what a child has completed* rather than *what a child has learned*.

As a reader of this book, you should be aware that the purpose of an assignment, quiz, test, or project likely determines how a teacher chooses to score it. For example, in a traditional gradebook when a teacher enters a score of 7 out of 10 for a worksheet, these points are often determined by completion and/or timeliness. In a given week, your child's electronic gradebook may include scores for up to five worksheets, all of which are based upon completion and timeliness. On the other hand, when a teacher enters a score of 28 out of 50 points for a test, these points are likely determined based upon questions (or parts of questions) that are answered correctly and incorrectly. You may be noticing that historically, traditional gradebooks have often metaphorically communicated points for apples (completion) and points for oranges (learning).

"Scoreboard watching" can be problematic for parents because they may not be aware of the aforementioned different ways that points are used in an electronic gradebook. Because parents tend to focus on the current grade at any given time in their child's gradebook, it can become easy to neglect the purpose of each assignment and how these points are determined. When the current grade dips below a desired threshold, parents may consider contacting their child's teacher or having a conversation with their child to find out ways "the grade can be improved," which may not be related to filling any real gaps in their child's learning. With such a strong emphasis on the overall grade, the act of "scoreboard watching" may influence parents into thinking that their role is to look for any and all opportunities for their child to accumulate points. If an assignment was not turned in, resulting in a zero in the gradebook, "scoreboard watching" parents seek to reconcile the problem by encouraging their child to "turn it in" regardless if the points awarded for the assignment were based upon completion or learning. If a failing test score drops the current course average below the desired grade, "scoreboard watching" parents may scan the electronic gradebook for previous missing assignments or ask about opportunities to redo previous assignments. Because the emphasis is on the "score," points matter the most, whether or not any significant level of learning has resulted from accumulating more points.

"Scoreboard watching" can also be detrimental to your child's mental health. The constant pressure of someone (adults) always looking over your shoulder discourages students to practice, create, and innovate. Any misstep gets recorded and automated in a way that often beats the child to the punch in their ability to explain the context related to the score or grade. Steven Adelsheim, a clinical professor of psychiatry at Stanford says, "When our focus is always on being successful and getting the A, we're not allowing necessarily the room for creativity in the room to attempt things. There's already a great deal of pressure that they're feeling on their own and from their friends, and this potentially adds to it. It creates both stress and anxiety" (Mosley, 2018).

One perspective to consider comes from author Jessica Lahey's book, *The Gift of Failure: How the Best Parents Learn to Let Go So Their Children Can Succeed*. In her 2015 book, Lahey recommends that parents relinquish the responsibility of learning to their children increasingly as their students grow older. By high school, parents ought to be rarely monitoring grades, because constant monitoring by parents does not teach students to self-monitor their actions and hold themselves accountable. When parents do check their child's electronic gradebook, Lahey recommends they review it systematically, perhaps once per week, and in doing so, ask their child questions such as "Is there anything you want to talk to me about before we review your current grades?" The electronic gradebook has become a mainstay for most schools and parents, but it is a limited portion of the improved parent-child dialogue regarding their learning journey.

OPPORTUNITIES TO CONTINUE THE CONVERSATION

In the opening vignette, Caleb Jones's parents were confused when they did not see any numbers or percentages in his electronic gradebook. While the Joneses were aware of their ability to access Caleb's grades, the information the school was providing to them did not initially make sense. With the historical information noted in this chapter related to the changing landscape of education, Caleb's parents would know that the standards in his gradebook come from a list of state-required learning goals, often called "state standards." Perhaps less important to Caleb's parents, yet influential in the school's operations, is the fact that these state-required standards are the basis of statewide standardized tests. The scores of the statewide standardized tests are used as a major component of the school's effectiveness ratings, which are required by the Every Student Succeeds Act; therefore it is in the school's best interest to help as many students as possible *learn* these standards at a high level. With all this new attention, and often accountability, it is no wonder that schools are considering standards-based learning, grading, and reporting. While admittedly different for parents and teachers alike, the ability to communicate more clearly a student's current level of learning is a major benefit of 21st-century grading practices. In the past, parents regularly checking electronic gradebooks may have inadvertently focused their time and attention on what a child has *completed* rather than what a child has *learned*. Caleb's parents, equipped with this new information and a school choosing to implement a 21st-century gradebook that communicates learning, are now in a wonderful position to watch their child's gradebook for the right reasons.

Questions to Ask Students

- When your teacher recently entered (insert assignment name) into the gradebook, what was the purpose of (assignment name)?
- What have you recently learned from the assignments you completed during the past week?
- As a student, are you able to access your grades through the school's information system (electronic gradebook)? Do you understand the meanings of the grades you see there?

Questions to Ask Teachers

- If I am unsure if my child is completing daily assignments, where can I look in the gradebook to find out?
- What do the descriptions mean in the gradebook and how are they different from points and percentages? What descriptions, symbols, or marks will I typically see in the gradebook and what do they mean?
- How can I help my child learn more in the areas they are not currently proficient in?

Chapter 2

But the Old Grading System Worked for Me

Why Are Schools Changing the Way They Grade?

Making the transition from high school to college can be daunting for students and parents. Review the following scenario of a newly minted college freshman reviewing her first semester grades with her parents.

Stella Bartell, a college freshman, just completed her first semester at her dream college, a large public university in her home state. A high-flying high school student, she could hardly wait to log-on and check her first semester grades while on winter break and back home visiting her parents. A straight-A high school student, Stella had never had a high school course grade below an A–, so you could imagine her dismay when she saw her "Introduction to College Statistics" semester-one course grade: a C–. Her parents, Rob and Nicole Bartell, were equally as shocked, and Stella seemed quiet. None of her other four collegiate courses were as poor when it came to grades.

Rob and Nicole pressed Stella, "What happened, did you get a terrible professor?" "No," Stella murmured sheepishly. "Did you turn in all of your assignments and projects, and do the homework?" Rob stammered. "Yes, of course," said Stella. Nicole attempted to stay calm and pressed on, "So what's the deal Stella?" "Mom, I feel like I don't know anything in this course; so much of it was new and way harder than high school," explained Stella. "You knew that was the case, but you took both advanced algebra and calculus in high school and passed with straight As—surely that had you prepared for Introduction to College Statistics? Your advisor told us this is the course 60% of freshmen take," Nicole added. Stella paused, then slowly explained, "The tests were so daunting, and in high school when I didn't always do well on tests, I had my homework assignments and extra credit to raise my grade so you guys never knew or thought it was a big deal. I have always felt like a shaky math student, but the pressure of high school was to get all As, and as long as I was turning in every single assignment, and often getting extra credit for showing up to study sessions, I could maintain As. I am sorry, I didn't think it would matter to you." "It does matter to us, luckily you didn't fail this college course and be required to take it over again, not to mention, hire a tutor. As you know, these courses are expensive and we don't have a budget to be paying for additional credits. I don't know how you plan to major in business administration Stella. You will need a better foundation in math to be successful," added Rob. "I'm sorry Mom and Dad, I didn't want to let you down," Stella sobbed.

The situation of the Bartell family is all too common for families and students in post-highschool coursework in the 21st century. Students can struggle beyond high school for any number of reasons and oftentimes the reasons are interconnected. Sometimes students choose a post-high school institution that is not a good fit, or they don't feel comfortable socially. While other times students struggle with the newly found independence and without the confines of a formalized schedule and supervised support of parents, teachers, and coaches lack the executive skills to be organized for post-high school success. What might be most concerning is the number of students who feel that their high school course load was rigorous and preparatory, in particular for college readiness, and feel they have the high school grades to prove it. However, stories like the Bartells' are all too common because of the flaws of traditional grading, in particular *hodgepodge* grading, a concept we will detail in this chapter.

In this chapter we will:

- Provide a brief overview of hodgepodge grading and how it has failed students.
- Discuss the "real world" implications of standardized assessments and homework.
- Explain the evolving role of homework as practice.
- Explain how the type of learning is changing in school to reflect the skills and knowledge that 21st-century careers demand.
- Provide opportunities at the end of this chapter for you to continue the conversation with your child and your child's educators.

WHAT IS HODGEPODGE GRADING AND WHY HAS IT FAILED US?

Hodgepodge grading refers to the common and traditional practice of including most everything a student knows or does into a grade (Brookhart et al., 2016). This includes both demonstrations of academic and non-academic factors such as homework, tests/quizzes, attendance, participation, cooperation with others (group work), and sometimes even extra credit. Hodgepodge grading, also known as omnibus grading, is an accumulation of points associated with a letter grade (Marzano & Heflebower, 2011). Sometimes teacher's gradebooks might include categories or weights divided by the type of activity (i.e., quizzes, tests, homework, participation, attendance, etc.). Figure 2.1 demonstrates a sample middle school social studies teacher's gradebook in a traditional, hodgepodge-style gradebook.

Hodgepodge-style gradebooks, as depicted in Figure 2.1, assign point values to nearly everything. Sherry Adams, the student shown in Figure 2.1, is earning a D− with a 61.21% in the first few weeks of her middle school social studies class. You can easily see that while she failed to complete two homework assignments, resulting in two zeroes in the gradebook, she also received credit (and in some cases "extra" credit) for turning in a syllabus, donating a box of tissues to the classroom, participating in a group, and filling out her planner. A primary

Date & Gradebook Entry	8-22 Syllabus Returned	8-25 China Geography Worksheet	8-27 Group Participation: Civilization timeline	9-3 Box of Tissues donated	9-4 Compare/Contrast India vs. China worksheet	9-5 Quiz	9-7 Planner completed- weekly check	9-8 Asia Unit Test	Total Points	Current Percentage (Grade)	
Points Possible	0	20	10	0	20	30	5	80	165		
Student Name (Last, First)											
Adams, Sherry	5	0	6	5	0	21	5	59	101	61.21%	D−

Figure 2.1. Traditional hodgepodge-style gradebook

concern with hodgepodge grading is that a student's grade can be improved or worsened without any assurance of improvements or decline related to actual student learning. For example, within a hodgepodge style gradebook, a student's grade may improve based upon *doing* something, such as filling out a planner, without *learning* anything new related to the course.

Researchers Hochbein and Pollio (2016) found students' grades frequently included "credit for speaking up in class, maintaining tidy workspaces, wearing school colors, returning signed permission slips, and donating canned goods, just to name a few" (p. 51). While many parents, grandparents, and students will recognize, and sometimes even prefer such hodgepodge grading practices, little to no research from assessment and evaluation experts recommend it (Brookhart, 1991; Brookhart, 2013; Guskey & Brookhart, 2019). Prominent grading and assessment researcher and professor Thomas Guskey (2009) stated the following:

> If grades are to represent information about the adequacy of students' performance with respect to clear learning standards, then the evidence used in determining grades must denote what students have learned and are able to do. To allow other factors to influence students' grades or to maintain policies that detract from that purpose misrepresents students' learning attainment. (p. 22)

Teachers, too, who often replicate the teaching and grading practices they experienced as students, may favor hodgepodge grading without realizing it. Researchers Cross & Frary (1999) found " . . . that many teachers blatantly use grades based on factors such as conduct, attitude, and even attendance to control student behavior" (p. 1). Unfortunately, those grading practices can be fraught with judgment and bias while confusing students and parents on the true purpose of grades. These hodgepodge grading practices from the 20th century lead to one group of researchers suggesting that gradebooks too often include everything "but the kitchen sink" (Cizek at al., 1996).

These "hodgepodge" and "kitchen sink" approaches illustrate how inconsistent grades are from teacher to teacher. What is an *A* in one class might easily be a *B* in another within the same school. For example, one teacher might include attendance, group work, homework, extra credit, tests, and quizzes, while another teacher may only include unit assessments and completing a class journal. For too long, hodgepodge grading has been implemented in schools with an assumption that it accurately communicates student learning. Students can benefit more from ongoing and detailed feedback of learning rather than the arbitrary assignment of points for any and all classroom activities and assignments, as hodgepodge gradebooks document. Guskey (2011) summarized hodgepodge grading in yet another way, "If someone proposed combining measures of height, weight, diet, and exercise into a single number to represent a person's physical condition, we would consider it laughable" (p. 18). Moving away from hodgepodge grading practices provides parents with a more intentional and detailed understanding of their child's learning. The validity of grades can be highly affected when measures of academic and non-academic factors are combined into a single grade (Brookhart, 2013). If in a post-COVID-19 pandemic era, high school GPAs are the most consistent predictor for their relationship with college completion, parents should be acutely aware of the level of accuracy each course grade represents in relation to curriculum. The overreliance of hodgepodge grading techniques by some schools could be hindering students' likelihood of college completion.

In summary, hodgepodge gradebooks highlight the differences between teacher grading practices. While one teacher may include points for turning in a course syllabus, another teacher may not. Hodgepodge gradebooks include points for a combination of students completing activities as well as demonstrating learning. Further, parents should be aware that differences in the way grade point averages (GPAs) are determined exist between schools. Twenty-first-century learners and their futures are too complex and interwoven to be characterized by a single symbol, mark, or grade intending to depict in-depth learning and application when grades are derived from hodgepodge grading practices. Future chapters of this book will outline remedies for hodgepodge grading and suggestions for parents to recognize and leverage in supporting learning for their children in 21st-century schools.

STANDARDIZED ASSESSMENTS AND HOMEWORK: "REAL WORLD" IMPLICATIONS FOR COLLEGE AND CAREER READINESS

A great deal of information about student achievement is provided through the educational system today; but for parents, making sense of it all can be a daunting task. As state accountability metrics have changed, so has technology changed the landscape and cost associated with assessing students. To assist in making sense of test scores, project grades, and course placements, we feel parents need a better understanding of what "assessment" means and how they are used while also understanding the role of homework for improved achievement.

First, *assessments*, regardless of who develops or requires them (an educational company, state, school, or teacher) are an *evaluation of learning at a moment in time*. Many parents associate this with a test, but not all assessments are traditional tests and might instead be projects, performances, demonstrations, or portfolios of learning. Results from a variety of assessment modalities allow for the best holistic picture of your child's learning, so while state standardized assessment results may garner media headlines, understanding district achievement, and the role of daily homework assignments is crucial for parents. Assessment expert Grant Wiggins explains the interaction much like the importance of snapshots to a family photo album.

> A good test has a role to play. The language that we like to use is, it's an audit. It's a snapshot. You don't run your business for the audit. You want more than a snapshot, you want a whole family album. But the audit and the snapshot have a place in the larger picture. (Wiggins, 2002, section 1)

Standardized Assessments

Students today are assessed in K–12 schools at a level and frequency most parents would not recognize from their own school experiences. For most, standardized assessments beckon memories of #2 pencils, bubble-form answer sheets, booklets, long weeks, and special testing schedules for a once-a-year event. While some of that traditional assessment culture remains, most standardized assessments have evolved into digital versions that may include writing and responding, manipulating of objects, reading aloud, and much more depending on the age of the student and the content or skill being assessed. Furthermore, some online assessments are not static for each child in the room and are instead adaptive in nature, meaning the difficulty of subsequent questions or prompts depends on the ability to correctly answer the previous questions. Frequently, these assessments are administered by direction of local, state, or even national guidance.

Standardized testing, regardless of the rationale, continues to have a storied and, at times, controversial role in schools today. In some states, standardized test scores may impact the evaluation of a teacher (Pham et al., 2021). Tying funding to student growth or teacher effectiveness fails to account for the litany of contributing factors that could cause variance in

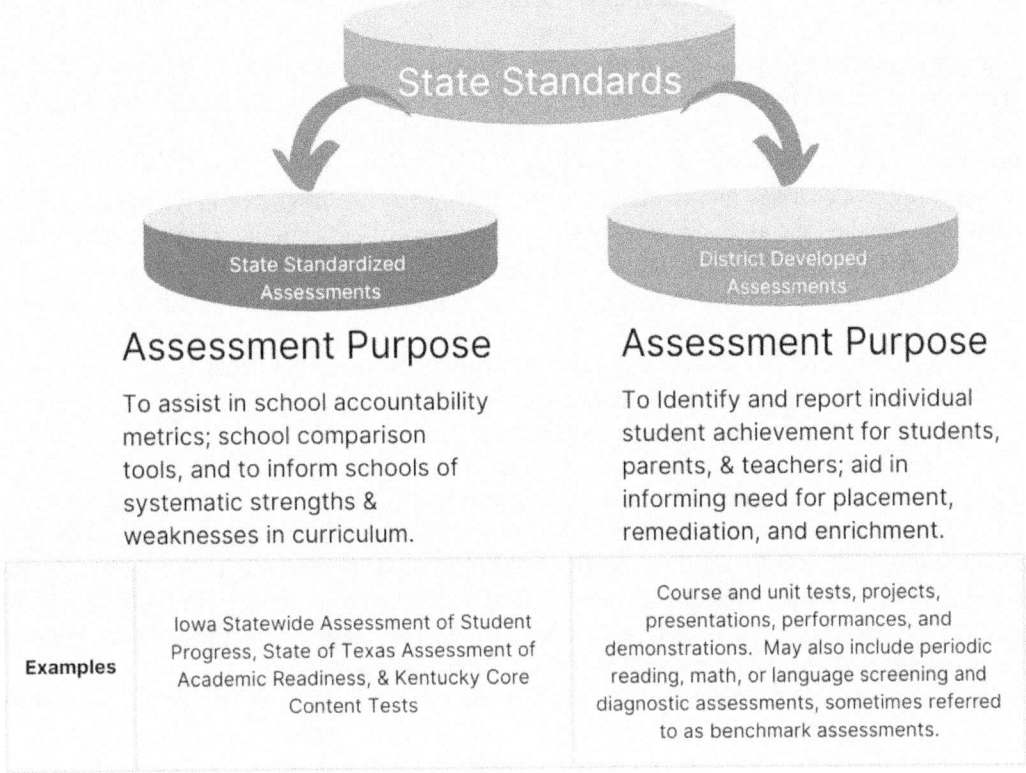

Figure 2.2. The role of standards for assessment

student achievement results such as socioeconomic status, race, geographic location, school funding, disability, etc. For parents, it is critical to understand the role of standardized tests and what they are used for within your individual child's school context. We offer two characteristics that answer the question "What makes assessment standardized?"

1. All students take the same or similar versions of an assessment.
2. All assessments are scored and evaluated in the same way.

The type of state or national standardized tests scores reported in the media and online are frequently lag measures of student achievement. Often given only once a year and typically in the latter part of the school year, the results, both good or bad, are provided to schools *several months later*, and therefore cannot be adequately leveraged in the current school year for adjustments. As such, parents should understand that standardized tests at any age are a snapshot in time, and while useful, should not be generalized too extreme in either direction to judge K–12 students' levels of learning.

In addition, what fits under the umbrella term "standardized assessments" is vast. From state or national achievements assessments to local, regional, or benchmark assessments, they all can serve a different purpose. For instance, many schools today may also use periodic screening and diagnostic assessments in math and reading to track individual student progress. While the delivery of these more frequent assessments may be standardized, the actions taken by schools in response to the results can vary widely from school to school. Generally, the results of these types of standardized assessments are not included in a student's grade, but are instead utilized for instructional interventions and an appraisal of school performance and accountability.

It is essential for parents to understand the difference between *normed-referenced* assessments and *criterion-referenced* assessments. Both types of assessments can be standardized, but for the purposes of this book, parents should ask their schools what type of assessments students are taking, and what the meaning of the results are upon their conclusion.

Norm-referenced assessments attempt to rank and sort a student's score in relation to all others who completed the assessment. Any assessment results that communicate a student's *percentile* is an example of a norm-referenced assessment. YAs a reader of this book, you might have experienced norm-referenced grading if your teachers or professors "graded on a curve." Norming for assessment purposes is challenging because a test score in relation to others, while interesting, can be a difficult measure of learning achievement depending on the subset of other students one is being compared normed against. In other words, norm-referenced assessments don't always give parents and students the full picture of their learning.

Whereas *criterion-referenced* assessments report what a student can know or do related to a body of knowledge, regardless of the performance of others (Bond, 1995). For example, most driver's license assessments are criterion-referenced. Regardless of how many people have "passed" the assessment, it does not inhibit the cut score or proficiency score to obtain a valid driver's license for the next person. Local assessments over school curriculum should be criterion-referenced. This means all students have an equally fair chance to score above or below the desired proficiency regardless of how their peers perform.

Norm-referenced models are not suitable for most K–12 school settings because the goal is no longer to sort and rank students based on individual learning topics like "evaluating algebraic expressions," but rather to ensure that all students achieve proficiency in these topics. In K–12 settings, it is important that all students demonstrate the necessary competencies for future readiness and success, rather than simply comparing their performance to a random group of peers in their course or grade level.

Most schools today adopt a more comprehensive approach to student assessment, which includes standardized assessment, regardless of format, as one aspect of the overall assessment process. This includes the evaluation of more metrics of student learning, such as local assessments (often tests), projects, journals, student portfolios, and demonstrations of state-approved curricular standards.

Two of the most common national standardized assessments are the ACT and SAT exams. In the past, these assessments have been a crucial portion of the college entrance formula. However, colleges and universities prior to the COVID-19 pandemic, began to highlight the inequities of over-relying upon criterion-referenced standardized assessments like the SAT and ACT for college admission (Lucido, 2018). Even before the pandemic, thousands of colleges and universities made such tests optional for student admissions (Bennett, 2021; Dance, 2021). In fact, one report suggests "the number of students who took the ACT in 2021 declined by 22% from the previous year" (Nietzel, 2021). This may beg the question, what then will be factors considered for 21st-century college readiness and acceptance?

In short, a more holistic representation of knowledge and skills. Colleges and universities review comprehensive portfolios for student acceptance, which include high school grades, essays, extracurricular activity involvement, evaluations by high school teachers and administrators, and even interviews. As the use of norm-referenced standardized assessments decline, parents must be aware of the increased importance both high school grades and the demonstration of non-academic skills will play in college acceptance.

Career Readiness and Grading

While standardized tests often focus on preparing students for postsecondary education, 21st-century grading practices often encompass separately reporting of academic and non-academic skills. Hodgepodge grading complicates this matter because it is difficult to isolate and intervene on which academic and non-academic skills individual students need explicit instruction and guidance to improve. Proponents of hodgepodge grading may argue that combining academic achievement with non-academic skills, like meeting deadlines and participation, does in fact prepare students for the real world, but unfortunately that is not the sentiment shared by many 21st-century employers (Hansen, 2021).

Parents may know non-academic skills as soft skills or attributes that relate to how a person thinks, behaves, and interacts with others. Most 21st-century employers would include skills such as problem-solving, teamwork, communication, adaptability, and flexibility in their definition of non-academic skills. It is not sufficient to assume that students will acquire the necessary skills for 21st-century employment through their family upbringing, K–12 school curriculums, or higher education programs without explicit instruction in these skills. Employers have increasing demands, and it is important to ensure that students are taught these skills explicitly. Non-academic skills are crucial for career readiness, and therefore should be explicitly taught by teachers. Accordingly, K–12 schools can play an important role in fulfilling that need by providing intervention on these non-academic skills through feedback; regardless of whether it is through an isolated grade or score. Parents should work with school counselors and other personnel to identify 21st-century employability skills they can support through their child's current curriculums and developmental stages. In Chapter 3, we discuss the rationale for this in greater detail.

Grading is crucial in communicating a student's learning as they near high school graduation. The importance of diversified course offerings that require the demand of both academic and non-academic skills that are adaptable to 21st-century workplaces are important. Grading systems that provide descriptive and accurate feedback will best suit students and their parents. It is natural to understand that parents' perspectives of grading might not match what they are used to, but it is essential that systems evolve to foster better alignment between student competencies and 21st-century career pathways. Knowing this, schools have also begun to reimagine the role of daily assignments to emphasize students' abilities to apply, reason, experiment, and innovate. To foster creativity and problem-solving skills, many schools are shifting towards grading practices that minimize the negative impact of errors in homework, which can have a detrimental effect on these skills. These skills are highly valued and are essential for success in the 21st century.

THE EVOLVING ROLE OF HOMEWORK AS "PRACTICE"

The purpose, tradition, and application of homework in K–12 education likely conjures a host of emotions for both students and parents alike. In fact, many of the parents reading this book will remember navigating the compliance maze that was their K–12 experience with homework. Some will recall homework that seemed impossibly difficult, other assignments that seemed irrelevant, and lots of worksheets! Perhaps many more parents than would like to admit had to navigate how to complete assignments late at night, on a bus home from a basketball game, or in the waning minutes prior to the bell ringing with some "assistance" from a classmate. Homework's intention is to provide practice, review, or preview of new learning concepts and skills. In many cases homework has done just that, but homework has often failed to achieve its altruistic goal and in modern grading systems, homework has been the focus of practice, whether it happens at *home* or not.

Initially, this notion may be difficult for parents to value because of how different it feels from their own student experience, yet years of research are quite clear on homework as it relates to learning. Simply *completing* homework or practice (compliance) has weak associations with learning meant to endure over time (competency) (Baker & LeTendre, 2005; Shepard et al., 2018). Beyond that, it is of poor mathematical and ethical practice to include practice or early attempts of learning when determining grades (Fisher et al., 2011; Vatterott, 2011). We invite you to refer to Chapter 3 for examples of student gradebook scenarios related to mathematical differences that combine homework and proficiency.

The purpose and quantity of homework in the K–12 experience should metaphorically mirror the journey of an entry-level employee and their evolution towards upward mobility. Elementary students, like apprentices and beginning employees, should complete practice but under acute supervision where constant feedback and individualization from a teacher or supervisor can be consistent and frequent. As a student moves into middle school, much like the employee who has now been on the job a few years, practice moves into the application phase. What new learning can be practiced and to what level to be better at skills and processes? Again, quantity and feedback will be differentiated but focused more on the need and autonomy of each individual. Lastly, as students enter high school, homework should reflect the practices of experienced employees in a particular field who have become highly individualized, independent, and intrinsically motivated in their work. This approach can help prepare students for success in their future careers.

The fruits of improved practice at this level are evident in their body and quality of work. If an experienced architect fails to stay up to date on the newest architectural tools and technology their likelihood of securing competitive bids naturally diminishes. Just as the architect begins to suffer the natural consequences of failing to practice learning on their own, so might the high schooler who blows off the assigned practice in chemistry when the chemistry exam rolls around. Homework and practice are tailored to the developmental stage of the learner and do not necessarily benefit from specific grades or the accumulation of grades of practice in the pursuit of mastering skills or concepts.

During your own K–12 experience, you likely completed many math homework assignments that resembled the following, "page 242, problems #1–43, odds only." At least once, it is also likely that you rushed to do all the problems all at once, right before the class period the next day, copied from a friend, or did not complete the assignment. Worse yet, it is likely that the assignment seemed more like busy work than a meaningful demonstration of learning, which creates more of a hoop to jump through than a meaningful practice event. This "get it done at all costs" model fosters a culture where teachers grade homework emphasizing completion over learning, which defeats the purpose of the assigned practice in the first place! Assigning a grading mark or score to assignments that were intended for students to practice neutralizes associated feedback for improvement and ultimately, learning (Schimmer, 2016). In fact, the blunt reality is that assigning a grade for homework at all is treating practice with extrinsic motivation, which is bad both for producing learning that sticks and overall performance (Lahey, 2015). To summarize, homework is an opportunity for teachers to identify misconceptions or errors in thinking, rather than a means of rewarding students for completion with grades.

Many parents and teachers during the early years of the COVID-19 pandemic were shocked at the dismal homework participation and completion rates. The pandemic further revealed a long-standing problem with homework: Homework assignments misaligned with what individual students need to master learning objectives. The lack of alignment can lead to fractured motivation and a host of other academic issues, none more important than students who do not end up learning the academic content and skills schools suggest they should learn in the first place. The amount of homework assigned is not always related to high academic achievement (Epstein & Van Voorhis, 2001; Epstein & Van Voorhis, 2012). In the words of Dettmers et al. (2010) "homework works if quality is high" (p. 467). Some might say another way, garbage in, garbage out. Because traditional grading systems conflate inputs (the "doing" of things) with outputs (proficiency), it is common to believe that completing more homework is always better. However, this approach fails to distinguish between the quantity and quality of work and can blur true measures of proficiency. To enhance outcomes with homework, the focus in 21st-century teaching and grading systems must be on the practice and feedback loops.

Twenty-first-century-grading includes consistent and meaningful practice for students along the learning journey, which may or may not include doing the "work" at "home." One problem may be in the very name "home-WORK." If your child sees the assigned practice as "work," they associate it with compliance and not learning. Ask most students why they are supposed to complete homework and take stock of their answers. We suggest the response ought to be "to learn and master the learning outcomes." Practice and homework should be diagnostic to the specific needs of students as they obtain feedback from their teachers. Grades are not the same as feedback when it comes to learning practice. Students can learn from feedback, but it is much harder to learn from a solitary grade or mark (Guskey, 2019). Within 21st-century grading, practice and homework, when given, are assessed, with feedback given but not "calculated" into the grade. Practice does COUNT—but it is not a part of calculating the determination of the academic grade.

Not including homework when determining final grades is different from past practice and may initially muddy the waters. Because 21st-century grading focuses on what students have learned, not a hodgepodge combination of completion points and points-for-learning, it does not make sense to continue including homework in final grades. Since 21st-century grading systems evaluate what students have learned, rather than a mix of completion and accumulating points, it is not logical to include homework in final grades. This concept can be confusing for teachers and parents, who may place too much emphasis on student compliance and effort rather than actual proficiency. When it comes to student proficiency in just about anything, everyone's path will likely look different. It is important to note that regardless of how homework has been incorporated into a student's grade, something that is nearly universal with parents and educators alike is the acknowledgment of the importance of effort. We believe 21st-century grading practices should communicate indicators of effort, but effort should not be combined with student proficiency of academic standards.

You may be reading this book and wondering, "In the real world . . . they won't have a choice to do what their boss asks them." In short, thinking about the real-world connection in this matter is more nuanced than it may first appear. Parents are right, employers will expect their employees to be competent in the skills and knowledge necessary to do the job. K–12 school, however, is not a student's "job." Through our experiences as teachers and administrators, we have heard parents suggest, "It's your job to get good grades." A more appropriate way of thinking through the role of school is first putting learning as the focus and consider a different phrase such as, "It is our expectation that learning be your focus in school."

The key difference when it comes to practice is that students are LEARNING fundamental and essential concepts and skills while employees who have been hired as adults are already expected to have MASTERED the skills and knowledge necessary to perform the job requirements. In fact, if employees don't possess the skills and knowledge they are often provided with the training and learning needed to be successful. That employers support considering early and developing attempts at mastering new organization knowledge and skills actually better parallels "real world" for K–12 students. Workplace knowledge and skill development efforts are rarely given demerits for quality while in training, but rather given real feedback and indications of where they need improvement (Littky & Grabelle, 2004). Expectations for adult competency are high because most people work in fields they already have foundational education and training to perform well before they start. K–12 students on the other hand, are constantly being challenged in skills and concepts in up to as many as eight contents at one time at a proficient level. Since all students learn different skills and concepts at different rates, it is important that 21st-century grading systems emphasize the most recent achievement that carries the most importance. Early attempts at mastery should not be averaged with later attempts of practice towards proficiency. It is natural that in the learning of a new concept or skill that early attempts may show lower levels of proficiency than latter attempts and thus makes no sense to calculate or average the two. This is why 21st-century grading systems do not take homework scores into consideration when determining final grades.

Using a basketball metaphor, if a basketball player skipped practice or didn't take the feedback from the coaches in practice and implement it in future attempts, feedback could be given to her and her parents on why her performance was not improving. Skipping practices (a.k.a. homework opportunities) has consequences that will manifest themselves in the game and thus is more real-world than many current antiquated grading systems that rely on calculating homework and/or using averages in grading. In those systems, where every practice (homework) is calculated and extra credit is granted, there is no intrinsic incentive to learn in a way that ensures the skill or knowledge will endure because of the fear of a "bad score." Consequently, students focus on completion versus learning. The concept of averaging practice with mastery gives a distorted image of actual competencies individuals possess. In Chapter 3, we will further illustrate the mathematical effects of averaging attempts of homework into a calculated grade as well as not valuing recency of performance compared to earlier attempts.

> Practice is practice and games are games, and while there is a clear relationship between the two, their purposes are inherently different. Practice is for improvement while the games verify the expectations and validate the decisions made during practice. (Schimmer, 2016, p. 81)

A final reason the use of homework in grades is problematic is students' varying accessibility to resources and supports needed to complete assignments at home. The COVID-19 pandemic rekindled discussion for teachers, students, and parents regarding student learning and new perspective on traditional views of homework. According to a Pew Research study in April of 2021, nine out of 10 students were required to complete some portion of their education in an online format during the COVID-19 pandemic (McClain et al., 2021). Unfortunately, it was also estimated that at least 30% of those students suffered little or poor-quality access to quality internet connectivity or devices needed to attempt and complete necessary learning (Schaeffer, 2021). This connectivity void has become known as the "homework gap." The homework gap was especially difficult for rural and low-income students, who often faced the connectivity challenge well before the COVID-19 pandemic.

The homework gap became an issue of equity when traditional hodgepodge grading was applied to the online context. Those students who had the time, means, and connectivity were more likely to complete homework and assignments that may have been tied to points or a completion grade, and those who were not, did not have such an advantage. Unfortunately, much of the homework and practice demonstrated by students who did have ample access to online connectivity, also had a wide range of support too, sometimes complicating just who all was involved in completing the task. Parents, often with good intentions, gave more of a helping hand to make sure a homework task was completed and submitted than making sure the student demonstrated independent practice with the necessary missteps and opportunity for teacher feedback and corrections. Schools that were already using 21st-century grading systems that focused on evaluating students' learning rather than just completion and compliance were better equipped to adapt to the challenges of online or hybrid K–12 education during the COVID-19 pandemic. Students were less likely to be disadvantaged by strict deadlines or internet connectivity dead spots for meeting arbitrary assignment deadlines. This helped to limit the stress associated with homework for so many students in an already stressful time of family illness, job displacement, and isolation. It is hard to argue any homework assignment is worthy or necessary for low-income high school students to find their way to a McDonalds parking lot in order to find free Wi-Fi to complete and submit such an assignment.

The evolution of standardized assessments, homework, and grading has been gradual, but necessary in 21st-century education. The systematic changes can be found from a federal to local level, and even down to individual teachers and classrooms when examining grading practices. Likely changes in assessment and grading are most noticeable to parents and grandparents today as practices tend to differ from their own experience. Traversing the paradigm shift can be more challenging for adults than students because they are less likely to have any other context to compare it to and are biased by their own experiences. We believe it is important for parents to recognize the differences and celebrate their evolution. All parents can start with monitoring how they talk about grades and shifting from grades as a commodity towards conversations focused on learning. As Vatterott (2015) stated, "In our relentless pursuit of the almighty A and perfect GPA, something got lost—learning" (p. 18).

THE TYPE OF LEARNING IS CHANGING: SKILLS AND KNOWLEDGE 21ST-CENTURY CAREERS DEMAND

In addition to reconciling the problems of hodgepodge grading, schools are changing grading practices in response to the type of learning needed to prepare them for the demands of 21st-century careers. In the late 20th century, globalization and increased connectivity of the world began to drastically change the nature of most traditional careers and vocations. In the United States, most careers, both blue- and white-collar, required a foundational K–12 education that was universal and appropriate to help sort and rank the future workforce of America. It should be of no surprise that metrics such as points and percentages became the central focus of 20th-century grading in schools. Metrics, such as the 100-point percentage scale, gave the perceived ease that students' academic ability could be ranked and sorted.

In the past, those who achieved at the highest levels in the K–12 setting were steered to a higher-education pathway while everyone else went directly into the workforce. For decades, going into the workforce with a K–12 education was sufficient to obtain a viable job and provide ample income and an adequate quality of life. As the 20th century gave way to the 21st century, so did the nature of work in the world as economies evolved towards more advanced skilled labor. The evolution of K–12 curriculums, training, and skills needed to meet the market demand did not follow in many countries, including the United States. Today however, in many instances, K–12 curriculums and standards, teaching methods, and grading systems mirror more of an economy of the 20th century than that of the realities of the 21st century.

Traditional school curriculums were delivered in more of a teaching model than learning model. Teachers taught most students in the same manner and in the same way regardless of the known individual student learning differences and abilities. In short, school was often more about what students could memorize from what was taught versus a promise to teach all students curricular foundations in a way that endured long-term. In other words, prior to commonly recognized learning standards required by state departments of education (outlined in Chapter 1), what was to be learned varied greatly from teacher to teacher and school to school. What curriculum was taught, learned, prioritized, and emphasized was highly variable. Frankly, for most of U.S. history, this educational program essentially worked and was not faulty in its general premise. School curriculums could be different and geographically tailored for industry and agriculture. Facts, dates, historical figures, and genus species names were essentially useless as an isolated memorized piece of learning for most career vocations, but those who had a propensity for memorization, navigating the social fabric of school—and for some, by pure luck—rose to the top. The curriculums varied and the way in which students were assessed and evaluated did as well, resulting in wildly inconsistent and incompatible grading and ranking systems.

Fast-forward to the 21st-century student who not only has most of the traditional "Google-able" curriculum items available at their fingertips, but also the reality of the disconnect between what is being taught and what the economy is expecting for the next generation of the workforce. This can be challenging for parents who once toiled over memorizing the 50 states and capitals or raced to complete timed math facts against their classmates. These seemingly "rite of passage"–type learning memories tend to challenge the parental mindset of, "It was good for me, it is good for you too!" This premise may be wrong on both accords. While it is certainly true, many 21st-century state academic standards require students to know rote-type learning such as the steps in the scientific method in science or Pythagorean's theorem in math, it is more often the case that the application, analysis, and justification of thinking and decision making will adequately prepare students for 21st-century careers. Vatterott (2015) found that the traditional A grade tended to represent an icon of discipline, responsibility, and hard work—which is commendable, but those skills alone are not always reflected in 21st-century careers. The goal is to get beyond learning as a means to an end, but to establish critical competencies that will endure for a child into adulthood that have cross-application benefits to both employment and life. Twenty-first-century jobs require critical thinking, sophisticated communication, non-routine complex tasks, and the ability to work collaboratively with others to solve problems (Friedman & Mandelbaum, 2012; Stewart, 2012; Vatterott, 2015; Wagner & Bhatt, 2021).

Historically, schools' grading systems often rewarded memorization of vast quantities of knowledge-heavy rote information, such as Spanish vocabulary words, world capitals, the bones of the human body, and the names of all the English explorers of the 1700s. While impressive, this knowledge is nearly useless today, if students cannot apply their learning to new, and sometimes novel, situations, problems, and applications. As you review Table 2.1, consider the differences in which students may have had to demonstrate their level of learning and depth of understanding in a traditional question versus an expectation in a modern assessment.

The use of hodgepodge grading and other traditional assessment practices is largely outdated and does not adequately provide the feedback students and parents need to support their path for future success. An overabundance of rote learning, simplistic assessment, and grading that may focus on regurgitation of facts has hindered the development of 21st-century skills found to be crucial to success in adulthood (Vatterott, 2015). Instead of just asking students

Table 2.1 Traditional Versus Modern Proficiency Expectations: Depth of Learning in Assessment Questions

Content Area	20th-Century Traditional Assessment Question	21st-Century Modern Assessment Question
Math	Round restaurant bill $24.55 to the nearest dollar.	Restaurant Bill: $18.55 + 20% tip = $____ Calculate the total bill for receipt and round to the nearest dollar.
Social Studies	What were the names of the generals for the Union and Confederacy in April 1863?	By April 1863, justify your opinion of the largest advantage remaining for both the Union and Confederacy in the Civil War.
English Language Arts	What did Fern do to save Wilbur's life in *Charlotte's Web*?	In *Charlotte's Web*, what do you infer both Fern and Wilbur learned about growing up?
Science	What are the three types of rock that most commonly exist in the glaciated region of the Midwest United States?	Explain how rock formation ultimately affected Midwestern home prices in 2021.

and children to memorize facts and perform routine tasks, schools and parents should strive to help them build on foundational skills and knowledge to facilitate deep learning in new and sometimes unfamiliar contexts. We all want students to be able to handle complex problems as adults, so it is crucial that they are able to apply their learning at a deeper level.

What Is Deep Learning and Why Is It Necessary for Success in the 21st Century?

A cursory study of the impact of the industrial revolution in history as it compares to the function of most schools today would be quite surprising if one were to stop and think about it. Consider the following. Masses of people attend a large site (factory or school) to learn assigned sets of content or skills and move through stationary settings (classrooms) by the ringing of a bell where attendance (clocking-in) is taken meticulously, and little autonomy is given to the attendees (students). It makes sense as the American school system was largely organized as a function to sort and rank students regardless of their predispositions or innate talents for competencies because the industrial economy only needed the "best and brightest" for management in the factory model. While it is overly simplistic to assume anyone who did not fit the "best and brightest" generalization didn't have a great deal to offer, they were able to find adequate employment to contribute to an economy and meet their individual and family's financial needs. Schools were designed to produce exactly what the economy needed. Grading of students in this model naturally followed suit. It was acceptable that not all students learned each content and curriculum regardless of what mark ended up on a formal grade or report card. In essence, learning was the variable for each student, but not time, which essentially was constant from learner to learner and content to content.

In the 21st century, student learning is characterized by a shift away from the industrial model, which emphasizes efficiency and standardization. Instead, the focus is on essential skills and content as the constant, and the time required to teach and learn these skills as the variable. This shift challenges traditional approaches to education and places a greater emphasis on the acquisition of transferable skills. The standards movement in schools has allowed for a better prioritization of curriculum and thus challenged the long-standing curricular theme, "more is always better." Students today need deeper learning and application of fewer curricular topics versus a conveyor-belt approach of the past where no one could ever truly know what was learned, and more importantly retained, for leveraging future success.

In the 21st century, the alignment between the goals of the educational system and the needs of the economy, which was present in the 19th century, has largely broken down. The fast-paced, skills-driven, and gig economy within the 21st century requires students to be able to demonstrate flexibility, adaptability, and context to knowledge in new applications. Where once teachers were the conduit of all knowledge, they are now the connectors of the traditional knowledge curriculums. Schools today need grading systems that provide timely and precise feedback, along with self-reflection, on students' abilities to demonstrate such skills needed in the 21st century. While knowing a great deal of "stuff" might be appealing to parents from a historical perspective, students are no longer competing in a knowledge economy, but a skills-based economic age. The advent of the internet and nearly instant access to information available at one's fingertips will require a new style of teaching, learning, assessment, and grading.

OPPORTUNITIES TO CONTINUE THE CONVERSATION

In summary, while it is tempting for parents to draw ire in the discrepancies between 21st-century grading systems and their monikers, one should find solace in the fact that compared to most traditional grading systems, these grading evolutions are clearer, more flexible, and more equitable for students. It is important to keep in mind that while standards-based grading models may have many derivations of each other, they are much more consistent and accurate than traditional grading approaches in which not only are grading practices different between every school, but they also often differ between every teacher in one school! The inaccuracy and invalidity of such practices do not help to paint an accurate picture of a student's true learning proficiencies that students and parents so desperately need to support student growth. Supporting student growth will often require parents and students to know the rationale, quantity, and design of student practice opportunities to best support their student in mastery of intended learning outcomes. To better understand students' mastery of learning outcomes, we suggest the following questions for parents to ask students and for parents to ask teachers.

Questions to Ask Students

- What have you gained in knowledge or skill through your practice or homework that you were previously unable to do?
- When you are given practice, assignments, or homework do you know what the goal of the practice is? Do you know how to find out if you do not?
- When you look at the feedback on your practice or homework, how can you tell if you are on track or not?
- What feedback do you get from your teachers or classmates that helps you feel confident about your learning?
- How can you keep track of what you know or can do in your classes/content areas?

Questions to Ask Teachers

- How can I use scores on practice, assignments, and homework to gauge my child's learning progress and determine if they are reaching the necessary level of understanding?
- What grade or content level application skills can we look out for in their current learning to support? (Such as problem solving, application, inferencing, justifying, predicting, etc.)
- If elements of behavior are included in my child's grade, can you explain to me how the behavior is necessary to improve the designed learning goal or target?
- How do I give positive feedback and encouragement to support practice in learning without relying upon external rewards?
- Please explain your understanding and approach to grading and assessment of learning.

Chapter 3

How Does 21st-Century Grading Hold My Child Accountable for Learning?

Consider the following conversation between a high school student and his parents:

Jared and Judy Smith are parents of Alex, a 9th grader in a suburban high school. While excited for their eldest child to start his high school experience, they are surprised as they begin to review the litany of course syllabi garnered from the recent back to school open house night. Each course syllabus from biology to algebra and physical education describes how their child will be graded for the upcoming semester, and essentially everything looks the same. To their surprise, there was *no mention of late penalties*. It seemed as if Alex could turn in all of his assignments on the last day of the semester without penalty!

"At first, I thought it was just a single teacher trying something different," said Judy. Jared chipped in, "After further review, we realized the grading policies were identical on every syllabus. Our biggest concern is that we didn't see any way Alex would be held accountable for his grade. We talked to a few other parents who felt the same way. While our children were generally good students, any teenager was susceptible to 'gaming' the system, which was really unnerving with college right around the corner," added Jared. "Fortunately, for us, we have a close relationship with Alex's band instructor, Mr. Harlow, and we picked his brain regarding this observation about grading at a recent community event. Mr. Harlow explained the essentials of what he called 'standards-based grading,' and while vastly different than what we were used to, understanding it made a big difference in our ability to support Alex at the start of his freshmen year," said Judy.

Jared and Judy Smith's introduction to elements of standards-based grading is a common, and often typical, introduction to pillars of 21st-century grading systems versus those of yesteryear. With an increased emphasis on learning, there appears at first glance, to be less of a priority on student accountability. In this chapter, we will consider common accountability-focused questions about 21st-century grading, such as "How do 21st-century grading practices prepare students for the real world?" and "How will this system motivate my students?" Furthermore, you will be able to compare the tenets of traditional grading, such as the use of zeros in a grade, and thoughts about student motivation when compared to 21st-century grading principles.

In this chapter we will:

- Provide a brief introduction to understanding accountability in 21st-century grading.
- Discuss the 21st-century grading implications of accountability for the real world.
- Provide an in-depth analysis of grading and student motivation.
- Provide opportunities for you to continue the conversation with your child and your child's educators.

UNDERSTANDING ACCOUNTABILITY IN 21ST-CENTURY GRADING

In schools implementing 21st-century grading, two practices stand out as being initial potential concerns regarding student accountability. The first practice is not penalizing students for late work. Within the opening vignette, the Smith family was surprised to see that Alex could turn in assignments at any time during the reporting period without penalty. Because there appears to be no grade deduction resulting from this student action, there may be a perception of the school being "soft" on accountability. In this chapter, we describe a different perspective on this practice, and why schools are choosing an approach that may appear to be counterintuitive. Rather than incorporating accountability-related penalties into the academic grade, reporting progress of employability skills, such as timeliness, are communicated separately.

The second practice is providing students with multiple opportunities to demonstrate understanding. If a student gets a C on a chapter test, a school implementing 21st-century grading practices may have a process in place to complete remedial actions prior to a student being provided another attempt to demonstrate learning of the concepts in that chapter. Once again, this practice may appear to be soft on accountability. From an outsider's perspective, students may be tempted to not try their best on the initial assessment to only procrastinate with a more motivated effort at a later date. In this chapter, we will describe a different perspective on this practice, too, and suggest how providing students a structured set of remedial steps actually adds to the rigorous expectations of a school. The chapter begins with a discussion of the real-world implications of 21st-century grading practices.

21ST-CENTURY GRADING IMPLICATIONS FOR THE REAL WORLD

You may wonder how 21st-century grading practices, such as removing penalties for late work, will prepare students for the real world. For example, one common rebuttal suggests, *"Well . . . in the real world, your boss won't be giving you unlimited time to complete a project or deadline."* While this may be true regarding some jobs or occupations, it is not a realistic comparison to students in K–12 schools. Students are not adults, and they are not completing assessments or projects for evaluation of their performance on topics and subjects they have already learned or mastered; like an experienced employee might. Author and lecturer Alfie Kohn (2011) reminds us that, simply put, "kids aren't just short adults." In other words, students should not prepare for the unpleasant expectations of adulthood by enduring them now. Therefore, your child's school aims to provide rigorous learning tasks and expectations that are developmentally appropriate and see students as learners, not just simply future adults.

One misconception is that because there are no points or grade deduction penalties for missing deadlines within grading practices, students won't be expected to meet any deadlines. Most schools who employ 21st-century grading practices account for meeting deadlines; they simply do not calculate or penalize the academic grade when they are not met. This means that an essential element of communicating to parents a child's academic standing is that academic and non-academic factors (i.e., timeliness and effort) are reported separately; not averaged together. When a school uses these grading practices, they are aiming to provide clear and descriptive feedback to students and parents about strengths and growth areas related to the learning goals. Consider the following example: 8th-grader Susan rarely meets deadlines but has a strong understanding of the learning goals in U.S. history class. The academic portion of her report card would communicate her *proficiency* of a learning goal such as "Analyze the difference between alliances in World War I and II." And within the non-academic skill section of the report card, she may have a *not yet* level of understanding for the goal of "Meets deadlines consistently."

Parents may mistakenly believe that non-academic skills do not contribute to a grade, when in fact they do. Within 21st-century grading, these skills are not mathematically averaged or calculated into the academic grade, but rather are communicated separately for clearer feedback to students and parents. Failing to communicate non-academic skill proficiencies separately can give a misleading impression of a student's overall knowledge and abilities as they relate to academic learning goals. When 21st-century schools separately communicate academic and non-academic skills, they provide a more holistic description of what the student can do academically as well as in non-academic areas such as meeting deadlines. Both are important!

Parents are right to be weary of a school's ability in preparing students for the real world, and should be encouraged to understand how 21st-century grading practices might prepare students for life after high school graduation. By separating academic from non-academic skills in the gradebook or report card, 21st-century grading demonstrates how a student's academic competencies and skills are complemented, rather than masked, within a single letter grade. Many 21st-century careers and vocations prioritize competency over routine compliance (Jerald, 2009). Thus, it is important that schools' grading practices assist in demonstrating the interplay between the dimensions of academic and non-academic skills. Most people today agree that one cannot maintain a job without being on time, showing critical thinking skills, working with others, AND demonstrating competency of the academic knowledge and skills needed to perform the job.

For example, consider the expectations that society has for highly regarded physicians. While most people appreciate a physician who is punctual and has a good bedside manner, they are unlikely to continue seeing a doctor who consistently misdiagnoses health conditions or fails to notice important symptoms. In this example, both non-academic skills (communication and timeliness) and proficiency in the profession (i.e., academic knowledge and skills) are important.

In addition to K–12 schools that report academic and non-academic goals separately on the report card, one common practice often stands out at the secondary level: providing students multiple opportunities to demonstrate their learning without penalty (O'Connor, 2017; Townsley & Wear, 2020). In elementary schools, teachers routinely provide remedial support to students who are struggling to read or learn mathematics. Yet, the idea of students being provided this same level of support, without impacting the final letter grade, seems to be different from what many parents experienced in their own school setting. The following section will provide you with an enhanced understanding of this redo and reassessment philosophy within 21st-century grading practices.

Redos and Retakes

Since most 21st-century schools have a responsibility to ensure that all students can and do learn, they need assessment procedures that accurately measure where each student is within their individual learning journey. When a first attempt at learning does not involve a student learning at a high level, the ethical and responsible thing for educators to do is to provide feedback and offer additional opportunities to learn. And when a student learns, they should not be penalized for learning a concept at a later time compared to their classmates, even if it involves more time or multiple attempts. In doing so, the student receives "full credit" for demonstrating a learning goal for the class or grade level. After all, not all of us learned to ride a bike, drive a car, or understand the stock market at the same rate. In the past, grade deductions (such as "10% off per day late" or redos to earn "half credit back") were used to show inadequate learning, but these methods have significant flaws in terms of both methodology and motivation.

A frequent concern with a policy that offers redos for full credit is that it may fail to motivate a student to learn the expected knowledge/skills the first time and thus promotes a laissez-faire, nothing-to-lose attitude for learning. Yet, research on intrinsic motivation does not support such a notion, and this is an assumption often made by many parents and teachers alike (Powell, 2011). The apparent procrastination or apathy is quite frequently emblematic of something else most teachers are attuned to diagnosing (Wormeli, 2006). Wormeli (2014) notes that "If an F on a project really motivated students to work harder, we'd have a lot more motivated students" (p. 28). Factors such as high engagement, appropriate instruction, and ample feedback are more effective determinants of learning success than completing practice in a prescribed non-individualized time frame (Guskey & Bailey, 2001).

Schools implementing 21st-century grading practices aim to avoid deductions or calculations penalizing for failed or lackluster efforts in attempts to accomplish the following ideals: 1. not dilute the meaning of the academic grade and 2. teach accountability and recognition for how deliberate practice can lead to enduring learning. In the perspective of students, the consequence for not doing the work, is doing the work. Permitting redos or accepting late work does not lower the bar but rather the opposite; promotes learning and accountability. This element of 21st-century grading practices sends a message that schools and teachers have a high bar for expectations and will not lower the bar due to poor decision making, apathy, or myriad other reasons that students learn at different rates. Author and teacher Rick Wormeli (2011) famously recounts one of his own students lamenting about the redo policy, "Mr. Wormeli makes you do it over and over again until you learn it. It sucks!" (p. 26).

When thinking about your child's school's philosophy related to permitting redos and reassessment, you may bristle with concern that such a system will reward apathy and fail to prepare students for real-world expectations. Yet, a better question to consider is whether we know that premise to be true in today's world. You may recount a situation in your own line of work, or that of others, when performance did not initially meet the organization's expectations. You likely received multiple opportunities to demonstrate improvement or growth, with feedback from your supervisor, before being assigned any type of penalty, dock in pay, or consequence in the workplace. Additionally, when an error or low performance was improved upon, upgraded workplace performances were not likely "averaged" with the initial less desirable attempts. Consider the following thoughts from international grading and assessment author Ken O'Connor on the redo and reassessment in education from the Nixa Public Schools (Nixa, MO) website, (n.d.):

> In a standards-based system, the emphasis is on learning. When a student doesn't do the work, the [natural] consequence is that he or she doesn't learn the content or practicing the skill. When we do not allow a student to turn in late work or re-do work, we deny that student the opportunity to grow character traits that are vital to student achievement, such as perseverance and persistence. If a teacher doesn't accept late work, the teacher sends the message that the assignment had little educational value. It's as if the teacher is saying, "Hey, it's okay if you don't do the work, and it's okay if you don't learn the content or skill." As professional educators working to prepare students to successfully navigate the 21st-century world, we can no longer accept these messages. Granting a reduced grade or zero doesn't teach responsibility to students who are not [self]-motivated. It actually allows the student to avoid the accountability of demonstrating what he or she has learned, and it teaches them to shrug off important responsibilities.

It is important to note that additional attempts to demonstrate learning by students is NOT synonymous with endless sets of opportunities, or as golfers might refer to as "mulligans." Instead, the intent within 21st-century grading practices is for students to be provided corrective instruction in between a finite number of attempts. A common misconception, when it comes to reassessment, is that a student has an advantage because they might already know what is on the assessment. This is erroneous thinking for two reasons. First, reassessments would be, at the very least, a different version of the original assessment reducing the possibility of students simply memorizing their wrong answers from the first assessment. This is a valid procedure because the assessments are designed to elicit student understanding of specific learning goals, which can be done in multiple ways. In other words, the assessment questions or tasks may differ, but they are designed to assess knowledge or skills over the same standards and at the same level of rigor as the first assessment, perhaps better thought of as an alternative version. An example of an alternative version of an assessment would be a teacher changing the numbers within the math questions while keeping the focus on right triangle trigonometry.

Second, it is a misconception that multiple assessment attempts are not representative of the real world. Countless high-stakes assessments, such as the Federal Aviation Administration aeronautical knowledge test (pilot's license), bar exam, ACT and SAT, and driver's test allow for multiple reassessment opportunities; however not without required corrective action. The opportunity cost for taking one of these high-stakes assessments again involves paying another fee and taking more time to prepare for the second attempt. Similarly, schools implementing 21st-century grading practices do not offer reassessment opportunities without an opportunity cost in the form of collaborative conversations between teachers with students that include a plan for reteaching, offering differentiated practice, and designing a roadmap for improved proficiency before a reassessment is offered and given. Some schools have gone so far as creating reassessment agreements or contracts that delineate a time, date, and place when a reassessment will be given and what corrective learning will take place prior to the reassessment event. See Figure 3.1 for a sample reassessment agreement. These agreements outline what the student and/or teacher will agree to and by when, before any new attempt at proficiency is permitted. Practices such as reassessment agreements have more real-world application, not less, when it comes to preparing students for readiness in learning and life in the 21st century.

West Middle School
Reassessment Agreement

Redos and reassessment are necessary to support student learning, regardless of *when* they learn at WMS. Reassessment comes with a "cost" for students, which involves submitting any previously incomplete assignments related to the learning goal, meeting with the teacher to discuss next steps, and completing any additional activities required by the teacher. The purpose of this meeting and these activities is to maximize the opportunity for students to demonstrate a higher level of learning on the reassessment. Meetings and reassessments will take place within three weeks of the end-of-unit/chapter assessment being handed back to students.

Student name: _____
Learning goal: _____
Meeting date: _____
Assignments that still need to be completed: _____
Additional learning activities to be completed: _____

Figure 3.1. Sample school reassessment agreement

Lastly, research indicates that teachers, like parents, wrestle with the benefits and pitfalls associated with redos, reassessments, or multiple attempts regardless of how formal of a policy their school may or may not have (Wisch et al., 2018). While teachers recognize the benefits of assessing the most accurate measurement of a student's knowledge or performance, they may be restricted through formal school policies (or lack thereof). The most important point for parents to consider is whether their child's grades accurately reflect their current levels of proficiency in a particular course or subject, and whether they are receiving an accurate depiction of the non-academic factors that often contribute to success and progress. It is important for parents to have a clear understanding of their child's strengths and areas for improvement to support their learning.

Schools must, of course, operate within parameters of formal schedules that include designated learning and assessment timeframes, schedules, and grading periods thus retaining some guardrails for both time as a constraint for learning and the ability to redo or reassess for improved demonstration of proficiency. Schools typically have calendars that are divided into reporting periods such as quarters or semesters, and policies for students to complete new learning through redo or reassessment may have practical deadlines to produce progress reports or report cards efficiently.

Online electronic gradebooks have enabled more real-time communication between teachers, students, and parents. In theory, electronic gradebooks should decrease the likelihood of parents being "surprised" by their student's academic standing in any one subject. The helpfulness of a gradebook for communication of student learning is only as good as the meaning and purpose of the marks located in them and the clarity they purport to provide. It would be appropriate and helpful for parents to connect with their child's educator(s) and have them walk through the meaning of marks and gradebook setup in the parent view, noting situations in which students were provided reteaching and reassessment opportunities. These access views are often different from that of a teacher, and most parents are surprised to know that unless a teacher is also a parent, they rarely see what the parent end-user view looks like in the electronic gradebook!

The Problem with Zeros

Perhaps no example of how the fallacy of extrinsic motivation and the consequences of traditional grading manifests itself better than the use of the zero in the student gradebook; in particular, if a percentage scale is being utilized. It is critical for parents to understand the role of the zero in their local school's gradebook, as it can have non-recoverable effects on student grades and motivation. Grading and assessments experts have long touted the ill-effects of using the practice of zeros in student grades (Guskey, 2000; Guskey & Bailey, 2001; Marzano, 2006, O'Connor, 2009; Reeves, 2004; Wormeli, 2006).

Schools implementing 21st-century grading principles believe the primary purpose of grades is to communicate what a child can know or do related to specific learning criteria and standards. Given this purpose, a zero in the gradebook would suggest that a student has learned nothing. More common, however, a zero indicates an absence of evidence. Yet, in practice, the traditional use of the zero is built on the premise that negative reinforcement and extrinsic motivation will activate students to do the assignment. This is rarely effective. If zeros were effective in motivating students to complete their academic work, these students would be receiving better grades with greater levels of compliance, and enhanced levels of learning in future years of their schooling, thus removing the necessity of this section of this book! Unfortunately, the same students receiving zeros in a traditional gradebook in 6th grade are often the same students receiving zeros in 9th and 10th grade. The tradition and practice of assigning zeros in grading is broken.

More specifically, the use of zeros within a traditional gradebook is problematic for three reasons. First, using zeros in a point- or percentage-based system is mathematically flawed. Second, the use of zeros dilutes the accuracy and validity of grades. Third, the use of zeros fails to intrinsically motivate students to learn and frequently has the opposite of its intended effect.

The use of the zero can be problematic, mathematically speaking, when the primary purpose of grades is to communicate learning. This is compounded in grading systems that prioritize points and percentages by way of averaging. In percentage-based grading systems where 60% is the minimum cut-off for passing, 60 levels of failure (0–59) are possible while only 40 levels (60–100) are for passing. This flaw becomes more evident when reviewed graphically in Figures 3.2 and 3.3.

High school English teacher Josh Kunnath demonstrates the 100-point percentage scale in a different visual manner to illustrate how many "levels" of failure are included in such a scale by replacing the percentage with its corresponding grade value (such as A, B, C, etc.). In Figure 3.3, Kunnath's diagram depicts the 101 levels of learning associated with the percentage grading scale. The essential problem of a 100-point percentage scale is disproportionality. There are 60 failing (*F*) performance levels and 10 performance levels each for *D, C, B,* and *A*. Using a percentage scale for grading learning is equally problematic.

For example, beyond mere point accumulation, most educators cannot explain to an American history student the difference in their learning between 62% and 67% at the end of a semester. A helpful analogy to better illustrate this issue is gauging the temperature of a room by that of using degrees Fahrenheit. Consider if you were asked to indicate how warm or cold it was in a given room using degrees Fahrenheit. Most would respond within a "ballpark" figure.

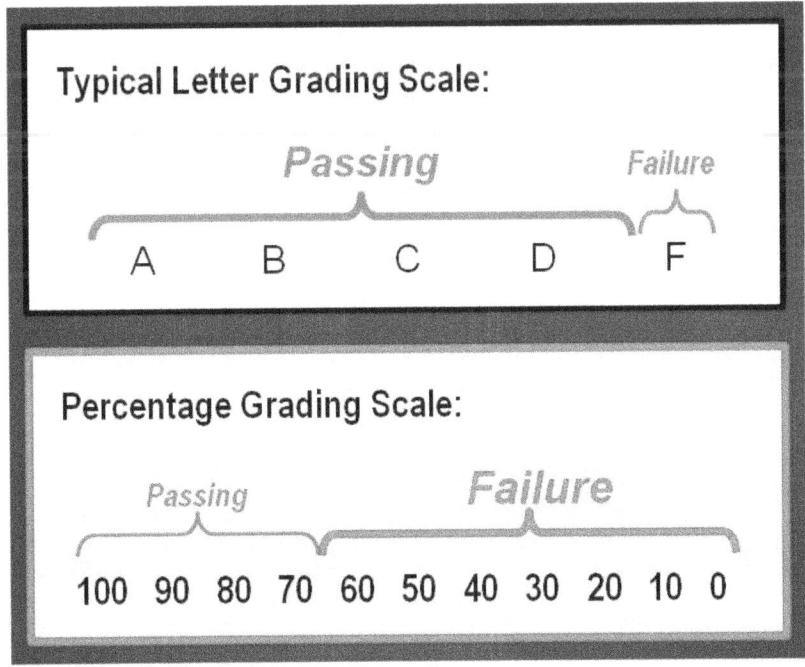

Figure 3.2. **A graphical representation of the percentage scale compared to letter grades.** *Adapted for presentation by T. R. Guskey from Guskey, T. R. (2015).* **On Your Mark: Challenging the Conventions of Grading and Reporting** *(Figure 2.1, p. 27). Solution Tree.*

Performance Levels in a Traditional Percentage Scale

A	B	C	D	F					
100: A	89: B	79: C	69: D	59: F	49: F	39: F	29: F	19: F	9: F
99: A	88: B	78: C	68: D	58: F	48: F	38: F	28: F	18: F	8: F
98: A	87: B	77: C	67: D	57: F	47: F	37: F	27: F	17: F	7: F
97: A	86: B	76: C	66: D	56: F	46: F	36: F	26: F	16: F	6: F
96: A	85: B	75: C	65: D	55: F	45: F	35: F	25: F	15: F	5: F
95: A	84: B	74: C	64: D	54: F	44: F	34: F	24: F	14: F	4: F
94: A	83: B	73: C	63: D	53: F	43: F	33: F	23: F	13: F	3: F
93: A	82: B	72: C	62: D	52: F	42: F	32: F	22: F	12: F	2: F
92: A	81: B	71: C	61: D	51: F	41: F	31: F	21: F	11: F	1: F
91: A	80: B	70: C	60: D	50: F	40: F	30: F	20: F	10: F	0: F
90: A									
11 levels	10 levels	10 levels	10 levels	60 levels					

Figure 3.3. Grade letter performance levels viewed through the traditional 100-point percentage scale. *Reprinted with permission of Josh Kunnath (2023).*

Perhaps one might guess it was 62 degrees when it was really 67 degrees. That is a pretty good guess, but still 5 degrees apart. If the thermostat was adjusted to 68 degrees, the guesser would likely not be more accurate because the intervals of temperature are so subtle it can be difficult to accurately describe the difference between each change, if at all.

Schools implementing 21st-century grading practices typically aim to replace the percentage scale with modified descriptors of learning (sometimes called "scales") with equal intervals between proficiency levels. Many schools utilize a smaller number of descriptors when communicating learning, in efforts to delineate the learning differences more clearly between the levels. In Figure 3.4, the school has agreed to communicate learning using the descriptors of *Not yet, Developing Understanding,* and *Proficient.* Equal differences exist between each level rather than disproportionate increments found in a percentage-based system.

The second flaw of using zeros in grading relates to the dilution effect it has on the meaning of the grade. As discussed in Chapter 1, the use of electronic gradebooks has exacerbated the problem of utilizing zeros because the grade calculation becomes hidden in the programming setup of the student information system. Often because the gradebooks provide a number down to the tenth of a percentage, parents or students rarely question their validity. Consider the following electronic gradebook screenshot for two students, Donald and Susan. The first gradebook setup in Figure 3.5 is when a teacher utilizes a percentage-based system and zeros for missing work.

In Figure 3.5, the gradebook scenario demonstrated both Donald and Susan achieved nearly identical scores throughout the grading period except for "homework assignment #2" and the final homework assignment, "Unit 1 Study Guide Assignment." In fact, Susan did poorly on both assignments and technically failed both attempts with a 59%. In this scenario, it's assumed Donald too "failed" those assignments because he did not attempt, turn in, or was absent for said assignments. For both students, the quizzes and assessments appear to demonstrate improvement throughout the grading period, but one major difference prevails at the end of the grading period; Susan "passed," and Donald did not. In this hypothetical scenario, the scores do not clearly indicate what was truly learned by each student. When comparing both Donald and Susan, it would be difficult to deduce a practical difference in learning at all.

Another setup in traditional grading includes applying weighted averages to types of assessments and learning activities when calculating the final grade. For example, homework might be 50% of the grade with quizzes/tests/projects as the remaining 50% of the grade. Refer to Figure 3.6 for students Donald and Susan in this type of gradebook arrangement.

Not Yet (1)	Developing Understanding (2)	Proficient (3)
The student shows an incomplete understanding of the learning goal with significant gaps.	The student demonstrates a partial understanding of the learning goal and has some errors.	The student demonstrates thorough understanding of the learning goal.

Figure 3.4. Sample schoolwide descriptors of learning

Date	8/25	8/28	8/31	9/5	9/6	9/11	9/16	9/17	9/21	9/22			
Assignment/ Assessment	Homework Assignment #1	Quiz #1	Quiz #2	Homework Assignment #2	Quiz #3	Homework Assignment #3	Homework Assignment #4	Quiz #4	Unit 1 Study Guide Assignment #5	Unit 1 Test	Percentage Grade	Final Report Card Letter Grade
Student Name (Last, First)												
Rose, Donald	48.0%	57.0%	64.0%	0.0%	76.0%	81.0%	83.0%	87.0%	0.0%	71.0%	56.7%	F
Thomas, Susan	48.0%	57.0%	64.0%	59.0%	76.0%	81.0%	83.0%	87.0%	59.0%	71.0%	68.5%	D+

Figure 3.5. A sample teacher gradebook, percentage-based setup

Date	8/25	8/28	8/31	9/5	9/6	9/11	9/16	9/17	9/21	9/22						
Category	Homework #1	Quiz #1	Quiz#2	Homework #2	Quiz #3	Homework #3	Homework #4	Quiz #4	Unit 1 Study Guide	Unit 1 Test	Homework Category Points Total	Homework Percentage Total	Quiz/Test Category Points Total	Quiz/Test Category Percentage	Final Report Card Grade Percentage	Final Report Card Letter Grade
Points Possible	10	25	30	20	30	25	20	30	30	100	105	50.0%	215	50.0%	100.0%	
Student Name (Last, First)																
Rose, Donald	6	18	21	0	24	20	17	24	0	71	43	40.9%	158	73.5%	57.2%	F
Thomas, Susan	6	18	21	11	24	20	17	24	17	71	71	67.6%	158	73.5%	70.6%	C-

Figure 3.6. Sample teacher gradebook, category weighting setup

In Figure 3.6, Donald and Susan are again in the same scenario as in Figure 3.5, except within a different teacher's gradebook setup that utilizes category weighting. Once again Donald fails to complete "Homework assignment #2" and the "Unit 1 Study Guide Assignment," leaving his homework percentage a paltry 40.9%. Susan did not fare much better on those same assignments, in fact failing both assignments, but managing to turn them in, unlike Donald. This resulted in Susan earning 67.6% of the homework points and when averaged with the 50% quiz/test category average of 73.5% Susan passed the course with a 70.6% C− grade.

In contrast, Donald was not so lucky and earned an average of 57.2% for a final grade when including his 73.5% quiz/test category average, thus failing the course.

As in Figure 3.5, both Donald and Susan scored the exact same scores on quizzes and tests, which once again beckons the question—is there a defensible difference in how these two students are graded when communicating true learning? Unfortunately, both gradebook setups prioritize quantity over quality. While being compliant, organized, and producing a lot of "work" may be highly valued by parents and teachers (and for good reason), these qualities should not be reflected so heavily in grades that they dilute the primary purpose of a grade, which is to communicate what a student knows and is able to do. It is important to strike a balance between evaluating students' effort and their actual learning and proficiency.

The third flaw of the use of zeroes includes the inverse effect it can have on student motivation. Mathematically speaking, this means, "to recover from a single zero in a percentage grade system, a student must achieve a perfect score on a minimum of nine other assignments" (Guskey, 2013, p. 71). The inherent rationale for the use of the zero is to punish and institute consequences to "teach a lesson" and encourage students to complete their assigned tasks, but because of the problems associated with averaging it quite often has the opposite effect.

When multiple zeros are used in the gradebook, passing a course becomes a slippery slope because students may see their grade as an unrecoverable and insurmountable situation. Instead of helping to mitigate apathy, the use of the zero may encourage further lack of effort, which may lead to students shutting down because overcoming zeroes becomes too daunting of a task. Put simply, the use of zeros for missing assignments does not motivate students to do better, but instead may send the message of them being "too far in the mathematical hole to meaningfully recover."

Understandably, the traditional use of the zero in a percentage-based grading system can stir up debate for both parents and teachers alike. Not calculating zeros on a percentage or points-based grading system seems like giving in and bailing students out, but when reviewed mathematically it cannot be considered ethical in determining accuracy of student grades. Parents are encouraged to understand the 21st-century grading practices related to zeros and reassessment with each course and teacher their child(ren) are enrolled. While you may not completely agree with every teacher's grading system, it is important to understand and interpret how valid measures of student learning are being used to support your child's education. Even if you do not agree with the specific approach being taken, it is important to work with your child's teachers to ensure that your child is receiving the support they need to succeed.

Recency Matters

Consider the following quote from Dr. Robert Canady in O'Connor (2017):

> Grades based on averaging have meaning only when averaging repeated measures of similar content. Teachers average marks on fractions, word problems, geometry, and addition with marks for attendance, homework, and notebooks—and call it mathematics. In mathematics we teach that you cannot average apples, oranges, and bananas, but we do in our gradebooks! (p. 172)

Traditionally, most schools rely upon the mathematical functions of electronic gradebooks to determine "final" grade. Additionally, the average (or mean) is often the most used central tendency algorithm for calculating a student grade. Averaging has many issues as it relates to communicating student proficiency of the intended course or grade-level learning outcomes.

The primary issue with averaging relates to combining practice efforts and early failures with more recent evidence of learning. In other words, students who can demonstrate their knowledge of accurately solving linear equations today, but struggled early on, are "haunted" mathematically by the inclusion of their initial poor understanding (low scores), thus bringing their average final grade down. Conversely, securing points on a daily practice assignment based solely upon effort might inflate the grade when a student lacks the ability to demonstrate learning on an end-of-unit assessment. Could you imagine a karate student who starts out as a white belt, practices, and improves eventually towards a black belt, but is only given gray belt status because their proficiency is averaged (Guskey, 2002)? We can't either.

Examine the hypothetical gradebook in Figure 3.7 to analyze both the flaws with utilizing zeroes and averaging performance. Each of the students are currently earning the same course grade but their journey in this math course appears quite different. Alvarez and Tony were slow starters but showed continual improvement especially in most recent attempts. Emily and Rebecca were quite the opposite. They started off doing quite well but began to trail off in competency. Sarah and Jamal are yet another story, both victimized by a zero at both the beginning and end of their grading period. This example demonstrates the lack of clarity of true learning for this course due to the pitfalls of averaging. "Grades should be based on a synthesis of evidence reflecting students' current level of learning or accomplishment" (McTighe & Ferrara, 2021, p. 59).

Schools utilizing 21st-century grading practices tend to find alternatives to the over-reliance on averages and employ trends, portfolios of evidence, logic rules, and/or mounting evidence to determine the level of proficiency, and ultimately a grade. Most of these measures have one thing in common—the most recent evidence matters most. While averages seem to be utilized so widely in everyday life, we rarely question the metric. Consider the following: if we could compute the "average" proficiency over the career span of a surgeon, plumber, pilot, or accountant—would you hire them? (Rose, 2016).

The strength of prioritizing recent achievement best supports preparation for 21st-century careers and vocations that rely on high levels of employee competency. Consider, for example, a veteran bank teller. A successful bank teller today cannot average great customer service reviews from the 1990s into their current performance assessments. They must sustain their performance in the present to be effective. In essence, one cannot average or "bank" their performance from the past. As it relates to 21st-century grading, teachers will often offer the opportunity for students to reassess a poor initial performance while keeping in mind that most

Student Name	Quadratic Formula Assignment #1	Quadratic Formula Assignment #2	Quadratic Formula Quiz	Quadratic Formula Review	Quadratic Formula Assignment #3	Average Percentage	Current Course Grade
Alvarez	59.0%	69.0%	79.0%	89.0%	99.0%	79.0%	C+
Emily	99.0%	89.0%	79.0%	69.0%	59.0%	79.0%	C+
Tony	65.0%	66.0%	66.0%	99.0%	99.0%	79.0%	C+
Sarah	0.0%	98.0%	99.0%	99.0%	99.0%	79.0%	C+
Jamal	98.0%	98.0%	99.0%	100.0%	0.0%	79.0%	C+
Rebecca	100.0%	99.0%	98.0%	49.0%	49.0%	79.0%	C+

Figure 3.7. Sample teacher gradebook demonstrating the problems with averaging. Adapted from Guskey, 2015

recent score matters most. It is hopeful with new learning and teaching interventions that the most recent proficiency score would be increased from previous efforts; however, if it is not, the most recent score could remain in the gradebook.

In short, efforts for allowing redoes, reassessments, and prioritizing *recency of learning* allows for schools to foster equitable paths towards proficiency, and rewards growth while promoting grit and resilience. The focus is not simply passing, but learning, and therefore schools implementing 21st-century grading practices aim to communicate these levels of learning as meaningful as possible.

GRADING AND STUDENT MOTIVATION

A myth commonly held by parents and teachers alike, is built on the premise that if students' homework, practice, or assessments are not scored using a numerical value (or "counted" for a grade) students won't be motivated to do their best or even attempt to complete them at all. The fact is, however, no research on student motivation exists to support this myth (Guskey, 2011).

Furthermore, research suggests traditional grading can actually have a negative effect on learning, and deter student motivation for learning (Guskey, 2011; Lahey, 2015; Ryan & Deci, 2020; Schinske & Tanner, 2014). This is particularly true for learners who struggle to grasp concepts early in the learning cycle and then are doubly punished when practice is completed at a later time compared to peers or not completed at all. This research affirms that teachers and schools should carefully consider how their grading practices are helping or hindering student motivation.

Grading policies should be established to motivate students to experience growth and learning. Traditionally, many schools' grading practices require teachers to grade every assignment, regardless of when it was completed and its purpose, and thus have created a norm of tasks intended to result in extrinsic rewards (points and grades). Without these rewards, students often do not see the value in learning (Dueck, 2014). In fact, using grades as extrinsic rewards sends more of a message that learning is something that needs to be endured versus something to be relished and enjoyed. In other words, learning is often something students have to do versus something students should want to do (Goodwin et al., 2023).

It will take students and parents collaborating to ensure that learning is the central focus of students' assignments and assessments rather than an extrinsic carrot-and-stick approach to grading using points and percentages.

The Perils of the Carrot-and-Stick Approach

Oftentimes, parents and guardians may recognize that completion, compliance, and even speed was compensated through grades in their upbringing and thus they expect the same in return for their children. Frequently, parents cite their own past lack of effort and success with those parameters as why they are so stringent with their own children. If you grew up in American schools prior to the 1990s, schools functioned in many ways as sorting mechanisms. Whomever could navigate the pathways of the education system by learning (or completing tasks), and often the fastest, were rewarded. This narrowly defined success system often was emblematic of the industrial world surrounding schools where creativity and problem solving were often discouraged and the highest value was on compliance, attendance, and consistency. As such, these are understandable feelings and, as previously outlined, are important and relevant when associated with the appropriate learning targets. Indeed, educators in schools should hold students accountable for meeting deadlines, taking ownership of their tasks, goals, and progress. However, it should never be done in a manner that leads to unproductive and inaccurate reporting of student proficiency of academic outcomes.

More broadly, this type of assessment of learning may not be preparing students for the realities of 21st-century learning and living. As Harvard researcher and author Todd Rose laments in a 2019 interview for *Harvard Ed. Magazine*:

> . . . we end up forcing our children to try and be the same as everyone else, only better. This cookie-cutter view of success limits our ability to develop the diverse talent that we need to thrive as a society, and it hurts our children. (Hough, 2019, para. 5)

Many analyses have outlined the necessary skills and aptitudes 21st-century students need to acquire to be prepared for success beyond their years in K–12 education. Often cited are those student skills of creativity, application, and innovation (Lahey, 2015; Wagner & Bhatt, 2021). If the assumption that traditional grading practices are outdated and potentially harmful is correct, it is important for both schools and parents to be aware of this and work to avoid using methods that may reinforce negative behaviors or discourage the development of 21st-century skills and qualities. Educator and assessment expert Rick Stiggins, quoted in Wormeli (2006), "Grades as motivators breed dependence, reduce risk-taking, creativity, and value" (p. 102).

Parents may recall their own rote demonstrations of knowledge or skills while sitting in a classroom of perfectly aligned rows of student desks. It is tempting for those recollections to conjure the initial thought on grading, "it worked for me." This, however, is a trap because we are all biased by our own unique learning journey that cannot be generalized upon a greater student population in the 21st century. According to psychologist and author Adam Grant, adults often have confirmation bias when it comes to grading. Confirmation bias is seeing what we expect to see (Grant, 2021). We tend to focus on grading and assessment procedures and policies that align with our own beliefs, even if they may not be the most effective in promoting student success. This confirmation bias can prevent us from considering new approaches to grading that may be more suited for the 21st century.

Most of the essential skills that students need to be ready and successful in later years cannot be taught or learned in a traditional manner. Additionally, traditional grading and teaching practices often encourage students to conform rather than encouraging diversity of thought, a skill that is highly valued by 21st-century employers. It is important to find ways to break away from traditional approaches and create learning experiences that foster creativity, innovation, and critical thinking. It is important to understand that the standards-based movement in American education since the early 2000s is not intended to *teach* every student in a standard way, but to account for every student to demonstrate *learning* of essential standards. If every grade level and content areas include learning outcomes essential to future student success, schools have an obligation to ensure all students meet the stated targets and nothing less. This is not to say all students can be the highest of achievers in all learning targets every time, at least right away.

The idea of essential learning can sometimes be misconstrued as a form of "trophy for every child." While it is true that 21st-century schools do not want any students to fail, they are not necessarily trying to prepare every student for the highest level of achievement beyond the curriculum. Rather, they aim to instruct, assess, and communicate learning in a way that better prepares students for the future.

Twenty-first-century schools utilize grading aligned to learning targets to communicate feedback of the student's current level of proficiency without the carrot-and-stick noise associated with extrinsic motivation of harvesting points, stickers, extra credit, and whatever else has been lobbed as a Hail Mary attempt to fire the motivational engines of students today. As best-selling author Daniel Pink, highlights in *Drive* (2009), carrot-and-stick approaches can give us less of what we want and more of what we don't want, ultimately working in the opposite direction of their intended purpose. These grading environments can lead to increases in cheating, apathy, resentment, inequities, and worse yet, a failed sense of creativity, autonomy, and competency in the learning process.

Schools and parents alike should aim to utilize grades to better portray progress towards learning versus extrinsic rewards. When grades serve as extrinsic rewards only, they can undermine deeper long-term learning, creativity, innovation, and motivation (Lahey, 2015). Instead, teachers and parents can use feedback from practice to identify competence and gain confidence in new learning. A student should never feel that homework, practice, or effort is useless because failure is inevitable due to a mathematical calculation (Brookhart, 2011).

OPPORTUNITIES TO CONTINUE THE CONVERSATION

Parents' familiarity with traditional grading practices, which emphasized power and compliance, may make it a challenge to fully comprehend 21st-century grading practices that focus on communication of proficiency. Like Jared and Judy Smith in the opening of this chapter, change seems to happen fast. Keeping up with all children's academic, social, and mental well-being can be overwhelming. However, research on motivation, analysis of the problems with traditional grading methods, and concerns about the validity of grades all indicate that improving grading practices is essential for 21st-century education.

It is particularly important now for parents to approach discussions with students and teachers about grading with an open and receptive mindset, as there is a need for clearer and more consistent practices that accurately reflect student proficiency. Author Stephen Covey outlined this philosophy well in the fifth habit of his wildly popular self-help book, *The 7 Habits of Highly Effective People*, "Seek first to understand, then to be understood" (Covey, 2020). Give both students and teachers an opportunity to explain why grading practices are being employed in the school and/or classroom. We have found the color brought to parent understanding through seeking to understand has most often reconciled initial grading concerns, while also solidifying an improved school-parent relationship.

Questions to Ask Students

- To what extent do your teachers explain WHY you are assigned specific practice, homework, or other assignments?
- In what ways do you know how to track and reflect on where you are in learning/demonstrating each standard, learning target or skill?
- If you need more practice or help learning a concept, what questions should you ask your teacher(s)?

Questions to Ask Teachers

- Where can I find the specific academic and non-academic learning goals for this course or grade-level content so that I can support my student's learning at home by asking targeted questions?
- How are academic and non-academic learning goals being communicated in the gradebook or report card?
- What should I look for in my student's practice/projects/performance that will let me know they are on target in their learning?
- What reassessment or redo policies do you have for students to demonstrate their most recent level of learning?
- What specific feedback and observations, not necessarily test scores or grades, can you share about my child's current level of performance?

Chapter 4

What About College?

How Do These Grading Practices Affect GPA, Scholarships, and Post-High School Positioning?

Consider the following conversation between a high school student and his parents:

As a junior, Ben is adamant he be allowed to take four advanced placement (AP) classes because they are weighted on a five-point scale versus the traditional four-point scale like most of the other high school courses. Despite advice from the high school counselor to balance his schedule, Ben feels he must prioritize his grade point average (GPA) to improve his class rank, and ultimately his chances for being admitted into a prestigious university. When Ben arrives home, he fills his parents in on the recent conversation with the school counselor, "I really want to attend a selective university and know that the courses I take, plus my GPA, will be taken into consideration, but I am not sure if my counselor gets it! He wants me to consider taking two AP courses this year and two AP courses next year." Ben's father weighs in, "Ben, you know that attending one of those elite universities would make your mom and I proud. At the same time, we both graduated from a state university, and we think you could get a fantastic scholarship to attend. Can you tell me more about this four-point vs. five-point scale thing and how it will affect your GPA?" Ben explains that he can earn higher than a 4.0 GPA if he takes AP classes because they are on a five-point scale, and the more AP classes he takes, the higher he can bump up his GPA and the better class rank he might be able to obtain. Ben's mother suggests he give his cousin Jared, a third-year undergraduate student majoring in civil engineering, a call regarding his experience at a prominent state university.

Ben: "Hey Jared, how is it going?"

Jared: "Great, odd of you to call, everything okay? You are usually a text message type of guy."

Ben: "Yes, but my mom suggested I give you a call and get some advice on high school courses to take. My counselor thinks I should balance my schedule and not take so many AP courses—won't I be at a disadvantage to get into the college if I don't load up my GPA?"

Jared: "Hmmm . . . Interesting. I used to think like you, but now that I have lived through three college years here, majoring in civil engineering I think I can be of some help. Ben, I met so many freshmen here on campus who thought just like you my first year. They bragged about their high school accolades, grade point average, and class rank. They said they were wanting to be engineers like me so I was intimidated at first, but it wasn't long after I was in classes with these students that I noticed they struggled, too. I was shocked. They had a hard time writing papers, explaining their perspective, and problem solving. They struggled to study and not be stressed out because they stayed up all night and crammed for major tests. I am challenged, too, but I feel like I have a better set of overall skills to be successful because I took balanced college preparatory courses in high school that helped me in math, reading, and writing, and I'm not just talking about AP courses! Some of these 'high flyers' have dropped out of the engineering program because they just couldn't cope with how to truly learn to be a successful learner of difficult courses."

Ben: "Whoa, I would've never guessed that. I guess my parents were right again. Thanks, Jared."

Jared: "No worries. College and the job market are always changing. Just stick to listening to your counselors, they know what they're talking about when it comes to being successful."

When schools use 21st-century grading practices, specific questions often arise related to GPAs, scholarships, and post-high school positioning. Organizations, such as the Mastery Transcript Consortium, and scholarly research provide a helpful foundation for parents to understand the effects of 21st-century grading practices on post-high school positioning, particularly at the college level. Previous chapters have focused on why gradebooks look different, why grades are changing, and how 21st-century grading practices address student accountability. Yet, as students progress through the K–12 educational system, we know that parents are becoming increasingly concerned with the "now, what?" If, as so many school district vision statements suggest, the aim of school is to *prepare students for their tomorrow*, then parents of high school students will need to understand the effects of 21st-century grading practices on post high school positioning, particularly at the college or university level.

This chapter addresses several questions that parents of high school students may have related to 21st-century grading, because we believe it is important for parents of K–12 students to feel comfortable and confident when their student eventually walks across the stage for graduation. Even though it may seem far off right now, we believe that parents of high school students should also consider the effects of 21st-century grading practices on their child getting *through* college.

In this chapter we will:

- Provide answers to common questions about GPAs, class rank, and scholarships.
- Discuss 21st-century grading and getting *into* college.
- Discuss the role of grading and student competency and getting *through* college.
- Provide opportunities at the end of this chapter for you to continue the conversation with your child and your child's educators.

GPAS, CLASS RANK, AND SCHOLARSHIPS

GPAs are a long-standing traditional calculation that attempts to provide a single number measuring a student's performance in high school courses. The most common way of calculating a GPA is to assign a numerical value, 1–4, for the final grade of each course. Partial points may also be assigned for plus and minus grades. For example, an A may be worth 4.0 points and an A– may be worth 3.7 points. This is sometimes called an unweighted GPA scale. See Table 4.1 for the numerical values that typically correspond to each letter grade, plus and minus, in an unweighted GPA scale. Typically, a student's cumulative GPA is determined by totaling the grade points earned so far and dividing by the total number of credits completed.

It may come as a surprise to parents that not all high schools calculate GPAs the same way (Vickers, 2000). Some high schools use weighted GPA scales. Letter grades for courses denoted as honors, college credit, International Baccalaureate (IB), or AP may be given a higher weight (Warne et al., 2014). For example, an A in an honors, college credit, IB, or AP

Table 4.1. Sample unweighted GPA scale

A	4.0
A–	3.7
B+	3.3
B	3.0
B–	2.7
C+	2.3
C	2.0
C–	1.7
D+	1.3
D	1.0
D–	0.7
F	0.0

class may correspond to 5.0 while an A in other courses corresponds to 4.0. See Table 4.2 for a sample weighted GPA scale. Note that weighted grade points in Table 4.2 are only for grades with a C and above. Some might argue that awarding more points for honors or AP courses provides an incentive for students to enroll in these classes (Klopfenstein & Lively, 2016). This thinking is that a B (4.0) in what may be a more rigorous honors class is worth the same as an A in an unweighted course. Still other classes award additional partial points (i.e., 0.2 or 0.5 added) for courses that are in between honors/AP and regular courses.

Acknowledging that high schools determine GPAs in different ways, parents should recognize that a student with a 3.76 GPA at North High School may not be an apples-to-apples comparison to a student with a 3.76 GPA at Metro High School. University of Chicago researchers Allensworth and Clark (2020) refer to these variations as "noise" in the GPA world which often makes it challenging for students at different high schools to meaningfully have their GPAs compared to one another. Variations for how schools identify and "weight" certain courses over others is typically not systematic within a region, state, and of course across the country. While GPAs are commonly used to summarize a student's high school grades using a single number, what this number represents and how it is calculated varies from school to school in what may often turn into an *apples-to-oranges* comparison. Said differently, "Grades can be seen as non-comparable across schools because they are based on criteria developed by individual teachers in schools with different curricula" (Allensworth & Clark, 2020, p. 199).

This *apples-to-oranges* comparison resulting from GPAs calculated differently at high schools is frankly, complicated. While it may seem like treating all GPAs that are weighted the same and comparing them to unweighted GPAs is a possible solution, further investigation into the intricacies muddies the waters. For example, for results from a survey of 793 high schools in Texas offering AP programs, 773 weighted AP courses within their GPA calculations, but within these 773 schools, some only chose to weight AP courses in science, mathematics, English, and social studies, leaving out AP courses within the domains of world languages and arts (Klopfenstein & Lively, 2016).

High school students themselves have even begun to figure out the inequities of GPA calculations and raise them as concerns to local administration. At Hamden High School in Hamden, Connecticut, students who take physical education as a summer course do not have this course calculated as part of their GPA, whereas students who complete physical education during the typical school year do have the course as part of their GPA (Friedman, 2022). For some students, including their grade, an A, in this non-weighted physical education course actually decreased their overall GPA. Students who completed the required physical education course in the summer did not have their GPA affected, which put some students at an advantage, not

Table 4.2. Sample weighted GPA scale

A	5.0
A–	4.7
B+	4.3
B	4.0
B–	3.7
C+	3.3
C	3.0

only in their GPA calculation, but also in their class rank relative to their high school peers. The lesson for these students at Hamden High? Take PE in the summer when it doesn't "count!"

College and university admissions officials are aware of this *apples-to-oranges* comparison between students at various high schools. This has led some universities to recalculate high school students' GPAs to level the playing field in their admissions decisions. For example, Miami University uses their own recalculation scale to "ensure equity regardless of the grading scale." Using this recalculation scale, Miami University (2023) and other institutions of higher learning may override local high school GPA calculations in favor of a scale they believe better enables them to create an apples-to-apples comparison. Yet, we know that no recalculation scale can truly encapsulate all of the variables that go into a student's final grade. These recalculations may be done in the spirit of admissions office efficiency and speak to the variability of GPA determination between high schools.

Class rank is also a long-standing tradition calculated by high schools and reported on the high school transcript as part of the higher education admissions decision-making process. First, it is important to understand what class rank is and what class rank is not. In most high schools, students are ranked based upon their GPAs. Student(s) with the highest GPA rank as first in the class followed by the student with the next best GPA. A student with a 3.80 GPA has a higher class rank than a student in the same school with a 3.79 or 3.56 GPA. Yet, that same student with a 3.80 GPA may have an entirely different class rank than a student with a 3.80 GPA at a different high school. With this enhanced knowledge of class rank in mind, you can likely envision a scenario in which a senior at East High School with a GPA of 3.95 and a class rank of 10 while a senior at West High School with the same 3.95 GPA has a different class rank due to how they compares to the students in the graduating class. Because class rank only communicates a student's *relative standing compared to their peers at the same school*, it is a metric without much inherent value. Alfie Kohn points out "The differences in grade-point averages among high-achieving students are usually statistically insignificant. It's therefore both pointless and misleading to single out the one (or ten) at the top" (Strauss, 2016).

Indeed, the National Association of Secondary School Principals (2020) has noted, "The current use of student GPA to calculate class rank has limited value in college admissions due to the fact it only shows student comparison within a particular school." A growing number of high schools in some states are no longer reporting class rank. According to the Iowa Board of Regents, nearly 20% of Iowa high schools do not currently provide class rank. Iowa's public four-year universities use a formula, called the Regents Admissions Index (RAI), which enables admissions officials to make efficient admissions decisions. The Iowa RAI historically included factors such as high school GPA, ACT score, and class rank. For a short period of time, students whose high schools did not report class rank were admitted through staff members in the respective admissions office making a case-by-case decision rather than depending upon the RAI computerized formula. Eventually, due to the growing number of Iowa high schools not reporting class rank, an alternative RAI was created that did not include class rank

(Iowa State University, 2015). As a side note, this change in Iowa public university admissions policy reminds us that the information high schools determine is useful to provide about their graduates on a transcript is what ultimately drives higher education admissions decisions, not vice versa.

In addition to GPA and class rank, parents may be concerned about scholarship implications when their school is first moving to 21st-century grading practices. On one hand, 21st-century grading practices minimize opportunities for students to improve their grades through compliant activities, such as turning in homework for completion points or taking advantage of scarce extra credit opportunities offered by the teacher. Yet, when parents consider how their student's grades are no longer earned, but instead represent what their student has learned, another perspective is warranted. One aim of 21st-century grading practices is to communicate more accurately what a student has *learned*. In this new system, a student with desirable grades is also a student who has learned a lot, which not only yields more opportunities for scholarships, but also enhances post-secondary readiness. These more accurate grades may also minimize students' ability to complete remedial courses, because their grades are based upon what they know and are able to do.

GETTING INTO COLLEGE

As a parent (or future parent) of a high school student, you may wonder if your child will be able to get into college. It is important for parents to know what college admissions officials value within the admissions process. According to the National Association for College Admission Counseling (NACAC), a variety of factors are important within the college admissions process. Within their 2019 report, NACAC found that over half of the colleges surveyed place considerable importance on grades in all courses, grades in college prep courses, and strength of the curriculum (Clinedinst, 2019). Private colleges placed relatively more emphasis on a student's writing sample and/or interview when compared to their public college counterparts. Yet, public colleges placed more emphasis on the ACT and SAT test scores. More selective colleges also placed a stronger emphasis on a student's writing sample, teacher recommendation, and extracurricular or work activities. This report admittedly is only able to share trends; however, the specific factors each college or university weigh when making an admissions decision vary greatly even *within* these public and private categories. As such, we propose that a high school student who knows *how to learn* (which may or may not be the same as lots of As and Bs on a high school transcript) will be well prepared to get into college.

One parent reflected upon how his children focused more on learning than merely grades when he shared a new perspective on what learning looks like in high school, "It's no longer 'I got an A on that,' but a different way of 'interacting and taking ownership over your own learning.'" Yet, the information schools provide about learning is different; therefore, it is natural to wonder about the implications for college admittance. After all, the *proficient, progressing*, 3s, or 4s in your child's gradebook are not likely the type of information that college admissions officers are familiar with! You should know that nearly every high school we know implementing 21st-century grading practices continues to determine a letter grade at the end of each quarter, trimester, and/or semester. Course letter grades and GPAs continue to be listed on each student's high school transcript, so that college admissions officials can process applications in an efficient manner. Based upon in-depth interviews with admissions officials, it is this efficiency in making admissions decisions that drives their inordinate trust in grades and college admissions test scores (Buckmiller & Peters, 2018).

We have personally seen parents share narratives in conversation and on social media suggesting that 21st-century grading practices have put their students at a disadvantage in the higher education admissions process, and this is simply not true. Instead, higher education officials from across the country have confirmed that 21st-century grading practices are on the same level as more traditional grading practices as it relates to the admissions process.

For example, in 2015, the New England Board of Higher Education and the New England Secondary School Consortium convened a meeting of admissions officials from highly selective New England colleges and universities. At this meeting, these admissions officials confirmed that students coming from proficiency-based high schools will not be disadvantaged during the admissions process (Blauth & Hadjian, 2016), a theme confirmed by Buckmiller and Peters (2018) in their conversations with admissions officials in the Midwest.

While nearly every high school using 21st-century grading practices continues to report letter grades and GPAs on a student's transcript, some schools affiliated with the Mastery Transcript Consortium (MTC) have started to think differently about what a transcript could look like without letter grades. In some early iterations of a "mastery" transcript, the MTC has suggested that providing colleges with more detailed information about the student on their transcript may be of benefit to both the student and the higher education institution. Schools using the MTC do not "reduce learners to single numbers, but they do hold them to high standards" and the transcript communicates mastery credits, which "combine to create a clear, succinct visualization of each learner's unique strengths." The MTC is a "better mode of communication for students as they share their interests, skills and strengths with colleges" and in doing so, the MTC experience enables students to share more detailed information with prospective colleges compared to a more traditional transcript.

Non-traditional college transcripts are not new within college admissions offices. In fact, admissions officials have cited home-schooled students who were carefully admitted without a traditional GPA (Buckmiller & Peters, 2018). The Frequently Asked Questions page of MTC's website (2021) notes "Hundreds of admissions offices have already received Mastery Transcripts and many more will continue to receive one as part of a student's college application. There has not been a single admissions officer who has said they can't use the Mastery Transcript in their admissions process." In the event your child's high school is thinking about moving away from a transcript that includes letter grades and GPAs, you can rest assured that a precedent has already been set within the admissions offices at institutions of higher learning across the country.

When thinking about getting into college, *cost* is often a point of conversation between students and parents. As the authors of this book, we see firsthand how much the tuition, fees, room and board at our own undergraduate alma maters have increased in the past decades. According to the National Center for Educational Statistics (2022), the cost of tuition and fees at public four-year institutions rose by 10% from 2010 to 2021. At private nonprofit four-year institutions, the cost of tuition and fees increased by 19% during the same ten-year time period. We anticipate that even before reading these statistics, readers of this book are aware of the increasing costs of higher education. These numbers do not take into consideration the rising price of textbooks, room and board, or other costs affiliated with being a college student. It comes as no surprise that parents of high school students may spend a considerable amount of time seeking answers to the question, "How can we (or my child) afford to pay for college/university?"

In her book *Indebted,* Caitlin Zaloom (2019) purports that "Middle-class families begin to face the problem of paying for college well before young adults sign their loan commitments. For parents the worries often begin in the first days of a child's life, if not sooner" (p. 2).

Zaloom's suggestion assumes that the cost of higher education is so daunting that taking out loans is a given.

One aspect of the cost of post-secondary education that is not often talked about in financial aid and other college preparation seminars for parents is the cost of students taking remedial courses in college. In the United States, research suggests that between 40 and 60% of first-year students at two-year and four-year colleges took a remedial course in English or math (National Center for Education Statistics, 2016). This staggering statistic tells us that about half of the students graduating from high school are taking a course over again while in college and paying tuition to do so. Sadly, if Johnny has a passing Algebra 2 grade on his high school transcript, there's about a 50/50 chance the college or university he attends will determine, often based upon a placement or other standardized exam, that Johnny does not have the prerequisite math knowledge to be successful in a college-level, credit-bearing math course that is required to earn a degree. The institution-developed plan for remediation involves taking Algebra 2, or, worse yet, first taking a course that precedes Algebra 2, that awards zero credits and does not count towards a degree's program of study. Instead, these zero-credit remedial courses are specifically designed to provide students with the knowledge they likely did not gain while in high school. As a parent, paying for a student's coursework when it is the same content taught in high school and does not directly count towards degree requirements, is, quite simply, a cost to avoid.

What if a traditional college pathway isn't my child's next step?

For students considering a career that does not require a four-year degree, such as vocational trades, their future employers may be equally as interested in employability skills rather than their ability to solve complex math problems or write a five-paragraph essay. For the past two decades, Bill Daggett (2022), international educational speaker and consultant, has been telling educators that our aim in today's technology-rich era is to prepare students for *their* future, not our past. Ten years ago, it would have been laughable to suggest that someone could make millions of dollars each year creating and sharing YouTube videos. In 2021, the top three highest paid YouTubers made a combined $300 million (Brown & Freeman, 2022). While these may be extreme cases of millionaire entertainers in today's social media space, these influencers represent jobs that were not imaginable a decade ago. Because the future occupation of students today is more unpredictable than ever, parents should also keep an open mind on the skills appearing in their high school students' gradebook or transcripts. Therefore, we posit that a gradebook or transcript that communicates much more than merely academic skills, a more composite metric or index, will be beneficial for the learner in the future we can only begin to imagine.

More pragmatically, recent reports from future employers of college graduates suggests that the skills and competencies they desire are less often related to the academic content and more related to these same 21st-century employability skills (often referred to as "non-academic" skills). Baird and Parayitam (2019) surveyed 50 different employers in the northeast part of the United States and identified 21 skills these organizations viewed as important for their future employees. Topping the list were interpersonal skills, critical thinking, listening, and communication skills. It is becoming even more clear today that employers want their employees to do more than reading, writing, and arithmetic. Imagining an educational system and corresponding grading practices that communicate these new competencies is what 21st-century grading practices aim to accomplish.

GETTING THROUGH COLLEGE

Teenagers (and perhaps their parents, too!) may be filled with thoughts and fears related to the GPAs earned in high school. These students may even think the 21st-century grading practices their school is using may somehow put them at a disadvantage for post-secondary admissions. As one high school principal recalled, "I don't fault students for that. But they're so consumed with a 3.85 [GPA] as opposed to a 3.75, they don't care *how* they get it. I tell them all the time, 'You will get into college, but that's not why we're here. We're here to make sure you get through college'" (Buckmiller & Peters, 2018). Recent research suggests that while factors such as high school GPA and college entrance exam scores may be helpful in predicting success in the early years of college, these same factors are much less likely to predict students' retention in college (Saunders-Scott et al., 2018). The results from some University of Chicago research illustrates that a higher high school GPA leads to stronger college completion versus that of standardized tests like the ACT and SAT (Allensworth & Clark, 2020), yet the variance between what comprises each school's GPA calculation can be far and wide, as previously described in this chapter.

Denning et al. (2022) found that at least one-third of all American students enrolling in college do not successfully complete a degree within six years. Other analyses have projected the odds of completion to be as low as one in two in the United States. In fact, some studies indicate that more than 68% of two- and four-year American college students need at least some remediation at the collegiate level (Chen, 2016). Much research and observation has been made regarding the concerning decrease in college completion and its subsequent causes, but often the issue of readiness and college preparation rises to the top (Bound et al., 2010). Parents are encouraged to not reflect on the number of assignments, assessments, and tasks completed as much as the rigor and quality of learning demonstrations their child can perform.

Schools and parents should collaborate to understand the intricacies of GPA, scholarships, and high school positioning. In doing so, the focus for the student should not merely be accumulating a portfolio that looks good in the eyes of admissions officials and those who award scholarships. If history repeats itself, good high school grades may result in paying for remedial college courses, which not only costs extra money, but also requires additional time before completing degree requirements. After all, getting *into* college is only a step along the way. Instead, we recommend that students, parents, and the school focus their conversations on helping students get *through* college. We end the chapter by providing opportunities for you to continue the conversation with your child and your child's educators.

OPPORTUNITIES TO CONTINUE THE CONVERSATION

While it is not uncommon for students (like Ben in the opening vignette) to get caught in chasing the almighty GPA, it is important for parents help to strike a balance for students in both their school workload in both breadth and depth. The K–12 experience is the prime period of a young person's life to develop and hone learning passions while exploring new frontiers of learning. If students see courses and their subsequent grades as only an end to a means, they are missing out on the joy of learning itself. We challenge parents to communicate with their children regularly about what current learning challenges them most. Parents should take inventory of themes associated with positive student responses and aim to communicate with school administrators, professional school counselors, and teachers to highlight opportunities to leverage growth in a balanced repertoire of both academic and non-academic skills necessary for 21st-century college and career opportunities.

Questions to Ask Students

- When it comes to your learning, what excites you most? What do you want to learn more about and why?
- What classes can you take in high school that will help you be successful while you are in college?
- What high school courses and experiences can you consider that will provide you with the study skills and dispositions needed to be successful in college?
- How could we/you meet with your professional school counselors to identify high school courses that would provide the best background of college readiness coursework regardless of major or university preference?

Questions to Ask Teachers

- How is my child's high school GPA determined? What does this mean?
- Does our high school determine class rank and if so, for what purposes is it used?
- What courses would you recommend my student take while in high school that will not only help them *get into* the college that they desire, but will also set them up for success in getting *through* college?

Chapter 5

How Can I Partner with My Child's School in Grading and Feedback?

Consider the following conversation between a middle school student and her parents:

David Murphy, a recently divorced single father of 6th-grader Sophie, found himself reeling in responsibilities within his new co-parenting custody arrangement. He was traversing uncharted waters, and keeping up with a 6th grader's academic success seemed a challenge, too. As David unveiled the first-quarter report card for Sophie, he saw myriad courses and corresponding numbers rather than the anticipated percentages and letter grades. He was puzzled by the sequences of twos of what appeared to be out of four, according to the report card key. "50%... 50%! I cannot believe this!" With the divorce recently finalized, David was hoping to avoid any new stressors for a while. Sophie had never struggled or received failing grades in elementary school, and so he asked her, "Sophie, why are you doing so poorly in your courses?" Confused, Sophie responded, "Dad, I am not failing any of my classes. I am getting twos, which is normal at this point in the semester. Most of the kids are getting twos because we just started learning about these topics. A two means *minimum proficiency* on our classroom's learning progression scale. Let me show you." Sophie logged on to her student computer and into a digital folder to show her father a visual of a learning progression scale provided by her teacher. "You see Dad, a scale explains what I can know or do at each level from one to four. A two is the same as *minimum proficiency*. I think I will be a three really soon in some of my social studies and math standards." Sophie opened the digital folders of social studies and math learning progression scales to show David where she had highlighted what she had already learned. Astonished, he asked, "Sophie, who highlighted that you know these items on this scale?" "Uh... I did Dad, who else?" smirked Sophie. Later that night David sent the following email to his ex-wife regarding Sophie:

Dear Patricia,
I hope you are well and thank you for trading weekends with me last month so that Sophie could attend her cousin's high school graduation out of state. She really appreciated that time with family. I wanted to let you know I had an interesting conversation with Sophie regarding her grades in middle school after reviewing her first quarter report card. I have never seen so much detail about what she can know or do. At first, I was caught off-guard, but when I listened to the ownership and understanding she had of her own learning I was proud! I hope she shares with you what they call learning progression scales in middle school and what she can know and do on them. It sounds like I should stay out of the way and let her lead! I am so proud of her communication and accountability. Here's some advice: Have Sophie share what this all means BEFORE you open her grade card, it will make way more sense!
Sincerely,
—David

This multifaceted conversation between Sophie, her father, and her mother, illustrates the value of parents who seek to understand the benefits of a 21st-century gradebook. David Murphy learned that a two means something much different to him and his daughter today than it did when he was a middle school student. Most importantly, this conversation illuminates the importance of students, parents, and teachers collectively communicating to fully express what is learning at school. When this communication triad is in place, the grade card, gradebook, or report card will serve as a confirmation of communication that has already taken place in the weeks leading up to the end of the reporting period.

In this chapter we will:

- Advocate for parents to celebrate and embrace transparency in the school's grading practices.
- Explain and discuss the significance of a communication triad for student success.
- Describe for parents a way to see the big picture and understand what grades are and are not.
- Provide a final set of opportunities at the end of this chapter for parents to continue the conversation with their child and their child's educators.

CELEBRATE THE TRANSPARENCY

As outlined in previous chapters, the context of a parent's own schooling experience understandably heavily influences their understanding, feelings, and perceptions of educational practices today, especially grading. From positive to negative and everywhere in between, we have proposed that traditional grading practices failed and often continue to fail to provide clarity for students and parents on how to interpret the meaning of a grade as it relates to the grade-level or course learning goals. Students (and sometimes parents, too) associated grading with people, not principles; thus beliefs, myths, biases, and even traditions ensued. This *person-rather-than-principles* mindset may have resulted in parents asking questions such as, "Which teacher was 'easier'?" and "Did Mrs. Jones provide a lot of extra-credit opportunities?" as well students asking questions such as, "Which courses best padded my GPA?" These broken practices focus more on earning a good grade than transparency in learning.

As teachers and schools change grading practices, parents should aim to embrace the transparency and clarity of learning tied to expected and published learning standards required by state departments of education. It will require parents to continue their own learning of not only teachers' instructional practices, but their assessment and grading practices, too. This is often known in the education field as becoming more *assessment literate*. Classroom assessment expert James Popham (2020) found that parents who are assessment literate are better able to help their children learn more successfully. Far too many parents reading this book have experienced assessments as a student, likely paper-pencil tests, that were given for the primary purpose of "giving" grades. It would be inaccurate and unfair to apply those same experiences to so many of the assessment practices used today because teachers are attempting to utilize assessment for a variety of purposes, not just grading. Twenty-first century assessment purposes include:

a. assessing a student's progress,
b. making instructional decisions, and

c. identifying gaps or strengths in learning to intervene or enrich individual student proficiencies.

The purpose of an assessment may or may not be determining a grade, so understanding the score or mark as a parent is crucial for clarity and communication. Schools and teachers have a responsibility to clarify which assessments and evaluation of learning are associated with the types of scores, marks, symbols, and grades parents are expecting regarding student performance, gradebooks, and report cards. While assessments may serve more than one purpose, it is imperative that assessments that assist in determining a final grade include only evidence aligned to the specific learning standards evaluated, nothing more, nothing less. The quality of the grade depends on the quality of the evidence elicited from a quality assessment (Guskey, 2015).

Parents in schools where 21st-century grading practices are taking place can expect to experience grading and assessment practices that exhibit consistency, standardized language of proficiency, and differentiated instruction to intervene and enrich student learning. The holdover practices of a 20th-century industrial school model can conflict with the values of individualization of student learning because they were not designed to provide such individualization due to the ranking and sorting mechanisms embedded in school practices. Continuing to practice such rigid, vague, and unclear grading practices fails to best prepare students for success beyond the doors of the 21st-century K–12 school setting.

Lastly, parents should also seek to understand and support communication and documentation that serves as success criteria for the course or grade level learning goals. Teachers likely use a variety of tools to assess and evaluate student proficiency. These learning assessment tools may include exemplar projects or papers, checklists, rubrics, study guides, and proficiency scales.

When parents have access and understanding for how learning assessment and evaluation tools are utilized to communicate learning, they can better support their students in conversations about goals and academic priorities. These documents and tools are often easily shared prior to the start of a unit of study and can help students and parents visualize success by knowing what proficiency looks like with the end in mind. Figures 5.1 and 5.2 are examples of sample learning proficiency tools. Figure 5.1 is a single-point rubric. This style of scoring tool identifies the criteria proficiency in the middle column while leaving blank space for teachers to provide feedback on the student's progress towards meeting or demonstrating extension of an individual standard. Figure 5.2, on the other hand, is a proficiency scale. These teaching and assessment scales assist students in seeing the complexity and application of the learning standard and what is required to progress to the highest levels of learning.

We encourage parents to ask their child's teachers for a brief orientation of how to interpret these learning assessment tools so there is common understanding of their utilization in the classroom. This transparency will lead to a deeper understanding of the school's 21st-century grading practices as well as strengthen the learning partnership between school and home.

THE COMMUNICATION TRIAD FOR STUDENT SUCCESS

Much like David and his daughter Sophie in the opening conversation of this chapter, a change in how schools, teachers, and students view feedback and reporting of academic achievement can be a difficult task to navigate. We have found, as both teachers and school administrators, that when parents have a full understanding of what the expectations are for both academics

Needs Improvement Inconsistent Evidence of Standard	Criteria Standards for Proficiency	Evidence that Demonstrates Extension of Standard
	Grip– Shake hands or continental; relaxed but firm	
	Footwork – For right handed player (reverse for lefty); on all forehand groundstrokes, dinks/drops, volleys, smashes and serve…weight on left foot. On all backhand groundstrokes, dinks/drops, volleys and smashes…weight on right foot (Law of Opposites).	
	Serve– Opposite foot forward; underhand motion; paddle lower than wrist; ball contact lower than waist; follow through to target; weight shift to target; recover to ready position behind baseline.	

Figure 5.1. A sample single-point rubric for pickleball technique in middle school physical education

Learning Outcome: Explain how the enforcement of a specific ruling or law changed society. *(Iowa Core Standard: 4th Grade Social Studies, 4.9)*

Learning Level	Criteria for Success
Exceptional 3	• I can accurately explain how enforcement of a court ruling or law changed society by citing specific social, cultural, or economic changes during a period of time.
Proficient 2	• I can accurately explain how enforcement of a court ruling or law changed society in a given period of time.
Minimally Proficient 1	• I can explain a court ruling or law that changed society.

Figure 5.2. A sample 4th-grade social studies proficiency scale

and non-academics, it is much easier for them to support their respective students in school. As students progress from elementary to middle school and then high school, the academic content and skills can be more elaborate, and frankly difficult, for parents to understand, but parents should not be disillusioned or disconnected by such concerns.

A common refrain from elementary and middle school parents regarding the difficulty of their student's homework and curriculum, in particular mathematics, is "I didn't even do this stuff when *I* was in high school!" While it is true that, in general, the curricular expectations may be more rigorous for students than in their parents' experience, it doesn't mean parents cannot play a successful role in supporting their student's success. Society and media have not done schools and parents any favors in their portrayal of what a "good" student is or does. Network television shows like, *Are You Smarter Than a 5th Grader?* and *Jeopardy* have ingrained an association of being "smart" with memorizing vast quantities of rote and often trivial information. The trap for parents to watch for here is known as the "illusion of knowing" masked by fluency (Brown et al., 2014). The illusion of knowing suggests that when a student can recite a great volume of facts and concepts effortlessly that parents, and sometimes teachers, can rest on their laurels. Regurgitating facts from a history class timeline or listing all the parts of an animal cell and its functions sounds impressive. Yet it will require some deeper prodding by parents to get a sense of whether students can apply and make sense of those facts to a higher application level of learning that endures long-term.

Parents need to feel comfortable asking their children how the content and skills they are learning in school could be explained to someone who doesn't know (quite possibly themselves!). Asking your child to explain a complex or confusing concept in 3rd-grade math, 7th-grade science, or high school sociology is, in fact, a great way for students to demonstrate deeper learning to their parents. If parents struggle with extracting information from their children about how learning is going, we suggest changing the question. If you are like most parents, you may have asked your child, "How are you doing in school right now?" and received short responses such as, "I have everything turned in," and "It is okay. We have three tests tomorrow." We suggest combating these typical brief student responses with questions such as, "Can you give me an example of a norm or value in our society you learned about in sociology?" In math, "Could you explain why you use a number line to solve these problems?" Questions that require students to explain, justify, or apply what they've learned are a great way for parents to understand how well their child has learned a given concept or skill. Understanding what your child is learning at school is a first step in partnering for student success. Once parents understand what their child is learning at school, comprehending the school's 21st-century grading and reporting systems will come more quickly.

The effectiveness of any grading and reporting system is how well it serves as a communication tool for students, parents, and teachers (Link & Guskey, 2022). We encourage parents to be active participants in understanding their student's grades and feedback when asking the right questions and communicating effectively with both their students and teachers alike. Ask teachers and schools for access to state standards documents, learning target lists, rubrics used in the classroom, or proficiency scales to have conversations about what your child can know or do (not how much or how fast they "earned" something) to support learning, not to criticize the system.

When it comes to grading practices, it is not uncommon for parents to have concerns about changes because they simply don't understand system procedures, markings/scores/grades, and even what a standard means in parent-friendly language (Burkhardt, 2020). This is normal and expected. In everyday life, we cannot regularly expect to understand all the inner workings and systems of professional organizations like schools. Medical charts, investment portfolios, car maintenance reports, dental X-rays, legal contracts, and even your cell phone bill need professionals in their respective fields to summarize and regularly communicate what reports and documents mean. We believe that parents, teachers, and students can all play a role in interpreting 21st-century grading and reporting systems. A meaningful understanding of these gradebooks and report cards requires a communication triad among these three groups.

A meta-analysis in 2015 of 37 different parent-involvement studies by Castro and colleagues found consistent findings for how parent involvement can positively be associated with positive academic outcomes. In short, their findings concluded that consistently two key practices were beneficial: a) setting high expectations for learning and b) maintaining regular communication with students. We believe that school communication for student achievement is not simply a two-way communication exchange, but rather a triad that equally includes the student.

Figure 5.3 depicts the communication triad for student success. The student, parents/guardians, and teachers are ideally in constant communication regarding learning. Too often, students are either exempt from the communication regarding learning or conversely, become the lone conduit of information.

Traditional teacher and parent communication has resulted in too much of an emphasis of lag measures for reporting student achievement and was often unidirectional. Report cards, take-home folders, and parent-teacher conferences are still commonly used today, but standard reporting measures like these alone need to be strengthened with more on-time, clear, and diagnostic communication. Traditional parent and school K–12 education communication is deeply rooted and can make it difficult to consistently collaborate to support and problem solve for student achievement and well-being. Infrequent quarterly grade reports and events, like parent-teacher conferences, don't alone grow collaboration; ongoing and meaningful touch points throughout the year do (Qarooni, 2022).

Fortunately, technology now enables appropriate use of e-mail, social media, apps, video recordings, electronic student gradebooks, and even messaging services for parents and teachers alike. These tools, while increasing communication for some, can also go too far. When digital communication is used solely in replacement of face-to-face communication within the communication triad, context too, can be lost.

The recommended triad for communication supports communication about learning, not just completion and grades. Grades are only one part of good school/parent/student communication and, at times, can be a distraction for a focus on learning (Erkens et al., 2017; Erkens et al., 2023). A hyper-focus on completion and grades over learning sends the wrong message to students that learning is merely transactional. A middle school teacher from Omaha, Nebraska

Figure 5.3. The communication triad for student success

(personal communication, December 29th, 2022), recently shared with us the following conversation from one of her students regarding a concern focused on a lens of completion versus learning:

> I recently got an email from a student asking me to update his grade before the end of the day on a Friday because he couldn't see his friends over the weekend unless he, "got his grade up." There is nothing wrong with parents expecting effort from their kids, but I think the idea of teachers being in control of their students' lives through grades gives the impression that grades just happen to students. Parents were using grades like currency. I sure didn't like that feeling.

Students who feel supported take more creative risks to learn, innovate, be engaged, and become intrinsically motivated (Henriksen et al., 2021; Kraft & Doughtery, 2013). The communication triad may, and often will, include scores and grades as a part of the communication regarding student proficiency and non-academic skills. We recommend that communication be as specific as possible. For example, a parent calling a 7th-grade math teacher should do this:

> I see that my child is earning a C– in your math class. Could you share with me one or two specific learning objectives I can support in a conversation with my son/daughter at home to help them be more successful?

They should not do this:

> Why is my child getting a C– in your class?

Parents and teachers communicating regularly models a collaborative approach towards goals, learning, and success for students. Furthermore, regular communication helps solidify increased trust and engagement between schools and parents (Bachman & Boone, 2022). If comprehensive teams of specialists (i.e., surgeons, therapists, sports psychologists, agents, and coaches) can collaborate for a professional athlete recovering from major surgery, we too, can foster collaborative approaches for students in their formative years of learning.

A note of caution for the communication triad. The problem with groups of three is that one of the three can easily feel left out or, worse yet, teamed-up upon. The triad of communication only works when trust and consistent communication flows in both directions for all three groups of stakeholders. Too often, students can feel that their parents and teachers are conspiring behind their backs regarding their achievement woes because of being excluded from the conversation. Additionally, teachers too, can feel threatened by a disgruntled student and their parents, especially when grades are issued, and clarity of grading marks are not widely understood. The goal of improved parent, student, and teacher communication should be to move from unidirectional communication and reporting towards opportunities to collaborate about co-constructing meaning, trust, and respect for a student's academic realities and goals (Dugan, 2022).

Long-time educator, author, and speaker, Todd Whitaker has for decades challenged teachers and administrators to treat everyone as if they were "good." What Whitaker means is to really assume good intentions. As school administrators, we have and do counsel teachers who have felt on the defensive regarding a student grade due to a tag-team of irate parents and their child who were not assuming the best intentions of their teachers. While teachers are human, and of course, not without faults or errors; we know of no teachers who awake each day, come to school, and assign grades with negative intentions. The toxicity of those relationships, or lack thereof, is in part due to how society has treated grades as a transactional act of compensation.

It takes a team to change the narrative and purpose of feedback and grades for the betterment of 21st-century students.

Jessica Lahey, best-selling parenting author of *The Gift of Failure* and teacher, in a 2015 NPR interview said the following when asked what schools and parents could do differently:

> Schools and parents need to stop blaming each other and work together to show children that we value learning. We can talk about the importance of education all we want, but our kids are too smart to fall for that hypocrisy. As long as we continue to worship grades over learning, scores over intellectual bravery and testable facts over the application of knowledge, kids will never believe us when we tell them that learning is valuable in and of itself. (Kamenetz, 2018, What Can Schools section)

COMMUNICATING WITH OTHERS "OUTSIDE" THE TRIAD: PARENTS, COMMUNITY, AND EXTRACURRICULAR ACTIVITIES PERSONNEL

The communication triad is essential to clear and consistent communication and feedback related to the proficiencies of students in all schools, but it can be enhanced by being broadened to the student's greater life context. Twenty-first-century parents interact both digitally and in-person with a great deal of individuals and organizations that help their children learn not only academic, but non-academic executive and life skills too. Think about the universe of learning a child can exist within today. From a daycare provider to a Boy Scout troop, a soccer team, to a jazz band ensemble, and the list goes on and on. The adults who sponsor, coach, and direct these groups play a profound role in the learning mindset of your child. While we believe learning from a diverse set of individuals, styles, and environments is healthy and applicative to the greater world around us, it can be beneficial for parents to have a conversation with these individuals about how they provide feedback, intervention, and enrichment within their learning contexts. To understand these feedback, intervention, and enrichment approaches, parents may need a brief one-on-one conversation with other adults or simply an observation in these learning settings. Understanding learning outside of the academic context will improve the parent's ability to draw connections between life's different contexts.

Take for example, Amanda, the parent of an 8th-grade student Eliza who loves participating in instrumental music and softball in addition to her academic school days. Amanda, much like many other parents, notices her daughter Eliza excelling and growing in her abilities to play the trombone in the school band as well as also playing first base for the softball team, but not as much growth or passion in math and social studies. By talking to the instrumental music director and softball coach, a parent might gain valuable insight into the learning of their child that they cannot see themselves. In this case, Amanda found out that in both instrumental music and softball, her daughter Eliza improved best when she had one-on-one feedback throughout a group practice. Amanda then communicated this to Eliza's math and social studies teachers through the communication triad with some ideas for effective feedback in the classroom. Specifically, Amanda found she could use analogies from Eliza's favorite activities to suggest how she could seek more one-on-one feedback in the classroom with her teachers. Her softball coach suggested that Eliza always seemed to slow down and focus when she encouraged her to "step outside the batter's box and breathe." This piece of advice worked for Eliza in softball, and when shared with her teachers they were able to adapt it to Eliza's nervousness surrounding classroom assessments.

Soon enough, Eliza's teachers were frequently and discretely reminding her to, "step outside the batter's box and breathe" and soon enough her mindset and achievement began to improve. It was not simply the mentioning of the softball analogy in math class, but rather the realization that Eliza understood the support network of a broader "team" beyond her mother and coaches.

Perhaps, one of the most powerful ways parents can support a culture of learning and not grading, point grubbing, and unnecessary academic competition is how they interact with the other parents and guardians inside their school ecosystem. As school administrators, we have heard countless rumors, inaccuracies, and perceptions from upset parents through email, social media, and in-person meetings. Many of these have been about grading. Through an investigation and conversation many of these concerns started with, "I heard from someone . . . " or "I read about it online. . . . " As a parent in a school community that supports a growth mindset, there will be moments where parents, too, will need to set the record straight. Twenty-first-century grading practices are grounded in transparency and clarity; and as such, if there is a breakdown in understanding, it is usually due to flawed communication between parents and the school. We hope the contents of this book provide you with talking points to better communicate both the *why* and *how* of 21st-century grading practices. The reality of the narrative regarding the culture of a child's school environment is a shared responsibility of both the school and the parents.

SEEING THE BIG PICTURE

Admittedly, it is easy for parents to get caught up in the day-to-day grind of accomplishing many necessary short-term tasks. Parenting today requires processing a great deal of information quickly; maintaining personal career needs; and still finding time to mow the lawn, buy groceries, and (hopefully!) spend some quality family time. Parenting often requires knowing the latest technology trends, paying attention to club and team sign-up dates, and keeping up with school communication as well as responding to volunteer opportunities. This is of course no easy task for parents with one child, much less, parents with multiple children at once. In their quest to be clear about what matters in their child's academic success, we challenge parents amidst the wash of information, deadlines, and expectations to *see the big picture*. When it comes to learning and grades, develop a long game for each child. Pushing too hard and over-communicating may inhibit the independence and resiliency a child needs to navigate learning on their own, while staying too far away, might foster a feeling of isolation or lack of support.

We encourage parents to utilize the communication triad to set goals for each school year or per course. Ask questions of both teachers and your child that are proactive and develop collaborative ways to improve accountability. A parent might ask a teacher at the beginning of the school year questions such as: "What unit or learning standard tends to be the most challenging for students in semester one?" A question for your child in middle school might be, "What is our plan for you to communicate to me/us if you begin to struggle in one of your classes?"

A long-term goal that parents, teachers, and society can agree upon is the ability for high school graduates to eventually succeed and contribute to society as an adult. We suggest orienting the communication of the child's growth experience, inclusive of their K–12 education, to be growth-minded with a focus on empowerment and intrinsic motivation. Traditional grading, which tends to overemphasize carrot-and-stick approaches, fear, and too much extrinsic motivation is detrimental to individual empowerment (Garlick, 2022). Parents should utilize the triad to discover how their child can feel empowered to take ownership of their learning through the school's 21st-century grading practices, and what resources parents and teachers could provide to supplement such growth.

"Permission to Fail" Rather Than a "Push for Perfection"

> We are all failures—at least the best of us are.
>
> —J. M. Barrie

Perhaps more troubling than the inaccuracy, inequity, and invalidity of some grading methodologies in the last 100 years of K–12 education that we have described in this book, is that many schools' grading practices have diminished a child's love of learning, innovation, creativity, and academic risk taking. Famed conservationist and author, Rachel Carson wrote about the importance of wonder in *The Sense of Wonder* (1965):

> I sincerely believe that for the child, and for the parent seeking to guide him, it is not half so important to *know* as to *feel*. If facts are the seeds that later produce knowledge and wisdom, then the emotions and the impressions of the senses are the fertile soil in which the seeds must grow. The years of early childhood are the time to prepare the soil. Once the emotions have been aroused—a sense of the beautiful, the excitement of the new and the unknown, a feeling of sympathy, pity, admiration or love—then we wish for knowledge about the subject of our emotional response. Once found, it has lasting meaning. It is more important to pave the way for the child to want to know than to put him on a diet of facts he is not ready to assimilate. (p. 45)

Anyone who has visited a kindergarten classroom in recent memory has likely observed the sense of wonder Rachel Carson so eloquently portrays. Students tinker, predict, explore, and most importantly, make mistakes. Their mistakes vary from illogical to emotional, but also in memory, sequencing, and patterns. Rarely are these young souls downtrodden from their mistakes and failures because of the rapid feedback and continued attempts of learning absent of grades. Gratefully, kindergarten teachers and parents have navigated the parent communication triad quite well absent complicated electronic gradebooks, convoluted metrics, and point grubbing. What happens when students and their respective parents get older and that changes? What can be done about it?

We recommend a thorough and ongoing conversation between parents and teachers regarding the differences between errors, mistakes, failures, and calculated academic risk-taking for the sake of learning and growth. Perhaps start with the words of John C. Maxwell in *Failing Forward: Turning Mistakes Into Stepping Stones of Success* (2007), "Errors become mistakes when we perceive them and respond incorrectly. Mistakes become failures when we continually respond to them incorrectly" (p. 18). In essence, failing forward is a change in mindset where failures and mistakes are separated from a child's self-worth.

As a child grows and matures, their natural inclination is to live in a world of social and academic comparison. As schools move towards more equitable 21st-century grading practices, ranking and sorting students becomes less valuable because the expectation is that all students will learn at high levels; hence the reason state departments of education have established the rigorous academic standards referred to in this book. The cellphones in our pockets, electric vehicles, and home automation devices, are more often a product of engineering mistakes, failures, and grit than they are of initial perfection. The saying "You learn more from failures than you do from your successes" is often cited as a valuable lesson, but we have observed that many parents are more comfortable with their children making mistakes in theory than in practice. In other words, they may be more accepting of their children's failures as long as they are not publicly known. This can make it difficult for children to learn from their mistakes and grow as learners.

Traditional grading, in particular the inclusion of homework calculated into a grade, fails to recognize the importance of productive struggle, experimentation, and tinkering. The mathematical expectation of traditional grading implies a push for perfection. Yet, first attempts of learning through practice, projects, papers, and presentations are rarely ever what the final version of learning proficiency ultimately looks like; therefore, parents and schools need to communicate how to replicate an entrepreneurial spirit without distinguishing the flame of creativity.

What is troubling about the "push for perfection" trend is that it leads to vast amounts of quitting and lack of resilience for students. In fact, their lives are riddled with easy opportunities to do so: Delete the smartphone app, restart the video game, switch to another club basketball team if they don't make the desired team, and the list goes on. When society is drowning in opportunities of perceived perfection, learning new content/skills that require mistakes, struggle, and on-going effort becomes more challenging than ever for students to partake. We encourage you to have conversations with your children about the learning process and how much is learned from mistakes and productive failures. This is more challenging for some parents than others, but we suggest that, as parents, you reflect on how you have discussed and framed failure (or plan to in the future!) with your children.

How have you navigated from the embrace of the falling child learning to walk and getting up again to where you might be today as it relates to K–12 learning and skills? It is important to distinguish between parents sharing lessons learned from their own mistakes and failures with their children and making decisions for children or taking actions to prevent them from experiencing challenges or failures altogether. The former can be a valuable learning opportunity, while the latter can hinder a child's development and ability to learn from their own mistakes. Often innocuous in intent, parents tend to intercede before a child has an opportunity to grapple with desirable difficulties, challenges, and errors. These moments are prime for autonomous learning and what is known as *consolidation* in their brain necessary for lifelong learning (Brown et al., 2014). In other words, consolidation in memory is imprinted by learned experiences.

We have heard some parents refer to these learning experiences as the natural consequences of life lessons. Practically speaking, Lahey (2015) challenges parents to not rush to school to deliver forgotten lunch boxes, missing assignments, or band uniforms when a child fails to bring it to school on a given day. While incredibly difficult for some parents, it teaches a required lesson many times over that not doing something simply won't do and contrary to the student belief, won't hinder them seriously in the short or long term! Parent for tomorrow, not for today (Lahey, 2015).

We, of course, don't advocate that parents seek failure nor embrace failure from apathetic behavior or behavioral missteps. Parents and teachers can communicate to distinguish student foolishness from errors of learning and problem solving. It is not just failures from acts of commission, but failure as an act of omission, too (Shoemaker, 2011). Many parents can identify the college-prep course they didn't take, the project or important test they didn't give their best effort on, or the choir solo they didn't try out for—and regret it. Conversations with our students regarding mistakes and failure often require a paradigm shift for parents and child alike, but 21st-century problems, careers, and economies require such a change. Parents often believe that by providing more structure, guidance, and influence by way of figurative safety nets that they are ensuring their children "stand" on the shoulders of lessons they as parents have learned, but paradoxically this can do more harm than good for student independence, grit, and resiliency (Lythcott-Haims, 2015).

When schools implement grading systems that support risk-taking, creativity, and multiple attempts at proficiency, parents should aim to capitalize on opportunities to inquire what their child is thinking and their goals for learning, even in the midst of temporary setbacks. Using the *language of learning* rather than prioritizing grades, scores, or marks will go a long way in establishing a school and family culture that grants permission to fail. Fortune 500 companies have found success changing the failure paradigm and embracing failing forward. Their success can be largely attributed to the culture of learning promoted by managers who do not punish for learning mistakes, and in fact embrace them, as they become the path to the next best product, procedure, or service. If Fortune 500 companies embrace, and in many ways require, failure in order to innovate, we too in K–12 schools can foster what failing forward looks like for students in academic disciplines.

When the school and parent focus start to orient more forward than backward, so does their feedback. Feedback in contrast to feedforward, whether it is included in grading or not, can be limited in its effectiveness because:

a. it's in the past,
b. it is not always efficient, and
c. it is usually negative.

Executive coach Marshall Goldsmith (n.d.) encourages feedforward communication to counter the ills of feedback. As parents, you do need to know how to compute the quadratic formula in algebra or be able to identify themes in a fictional text in middle school language arts to discuss and help design learning goals for your child. Feedforward communication is an essential element of the communication triad that fosters support, a growth mindset, and individual autonomy for students.

A quote that we believe encompasses a helpful parenting mindset towards grades is as follows: "Maybe what we should be telling kids is not that grades don't matter . . . but they're not the *only* thing that matters. Teaching them otherwise is a huge injustice to children" (Borba, 2021, p. 10).

A final course grade, at best, is a summation of proficiency at a moment in time, nothing more or less (Guskey, 2022). Learning is a continuum and is confined by artificial time constraints often known as quarters, trimesters, semesters, and so on. Too much stock has been put into scores, marks, and grades as accepted and valid measures of student proficiency. Without getting into the details of educational psychometrics, all scores, marks, and grades are an inference made from a presumed valid and reliable set of instruments (i.e., assignments, quizzes, or projects). These interpretations are aligned to curricular aims with the best intentions, but if these interpretations in the form of "points earned" are simply fed into a computerized gradebook and computed touting accuracy of student proficiency, parents are right to be skeptical. Traditional grades often fail to serve any single purpose because their meaning lacks universal clarity. Parents who inadvertently assign meaning to every assignment in the gradebook run the risk of confusion for their child, or worse yet disillusionment in their child's abilities. Albert Einstein once said, "Everybody is a genius. But if you judge a fish by its ability to climb a tree, it will live its whole life believing that it is stupid."

As parents, we have a natural inclination to feel like our children, with their flaws and merits alike, reflect our parenting, guidance, and even morals. While certainly much truth can be found in the nurture and influence of parenting, we have extended that too far in many facets of our lives as it pertains to grades, rankings, and percentiles. A child's grade in a particular course or grade level is not a direct reflection of the value of a person they or you are as a parent. Grades are not a measure of your child's worth or ability (Lahey, 2015). One-dimensional aspects of a letter or number grade can in no way begin to describe the multidimensional characteristics of your child. Labels become problematic and can often become a self-fulfilling prophecy that leads to apathy and failed motivation. We don't have "low" or "high" kids, nor do we have "smart" or "slow" kids because of a grade, score, mark, or symbol.

Grading reform and systematic school practices are not another fad for schools, nor is a new "agenda" item. In 2021, Howard Kirshenbaum, Rodney Napier, and Sidney Simon celebrated the 50th anniversary of their landmark analysis of the woes of traditional grading in their seminal critique, novel, *Wad-Ja-Get? The Grading Game in American Education.* This book illustrates the perils of traditional grading practices in the late 1960s that can sadly still largely be found in 21st-century schools. The title itself, *Wad-Ja-Get*, conjures a grading and assessment process that is faulty in premise and hurtful in the way we can use student grades to represent learning and proficiency. In 21st-century grading practices, students are not "given" grades and do not "get" grades per se, but rather assigned grades from teachers' evaluation of clear learning targets and set criteria for proficiency. Grading should not be posited or referred to as a "game" for teachers, students, and parents.

While there has always been teacher subjectivity in grading, and there always will be, grades are not given, they are indicators of learning at a particular place in time. Because grades are merely indicators, we find the following phrase to be troublesome: "Students don't get grades; grades are earned." Using the term "earned" is too closely associated with compliance and "hoop-jumping." Following the rules and meeting the expectations are important, but those alone do not constitute a *grade* in algebra, 6th-grade social studies, or 3rd-grade language arts.

This transactional relationship between student and teacher emanates from an era of K–12 education where grades were a mystery. Standards did not often exist, therefore it was difficult for students and parents to know where each student stood in relation to learning expectations. The targets, much less what proficiency towards them looked like, were vague and sometimes non-existent, thus when grades, scores, or marks were assigned by teachers, it felt like they was "given" to a student. Worse yet, since an industrial age demanded a rank and sort of society, some of those grading practices were norm-referenced (scored on a curve) thus requiring the teacher to do some calculation in relation to one another for a grade and not in relation to a standard set of learning criteria.

We hope those norm-referenced grading days are in the rearview mirror for K–12 schools. As previously noted, when electronic gradebooks and student information systems came online for parents to view, the feeling of "getting grades" still resonated because many parents lacked the context in which the grades were calculated. Often grades did not or do not represent valid measures of student proficiency and learning, and as such are no more accurate than they were decades ago, just faster in getting to the parent email inbox and often accompanied by an increase to the dial of the parent pressure cooker.

OPPORTUNITIES TO CONTINUE THE CONVERSATION

We hope that this book has enabled you as parents to partner with educators to identify numerous ways to enhance transparency, accuracy, and responsibility into the process of determining and interpreting student grades and grading processes. This overarching theme is not new. We know parents desire clarity and transparency when it comes to their student's learning. Link

& Guskey (2022) found that when surveying over 10,000 students, parents, and teachers, the cumulative primary response regarding the purpose of grades was: *grades should describe how well students have achieved the learning goals established for a grade level or course and reflect students' performance based on specific learning criteria.*

The purpose of this book was to assist parents and guardians in understanding what is involved in 21st-century grading and assessment. We believe this will enable you to become better partners with educators in efforts to understand your students' strengths and areas for improvement. Our aim was to help you understand how education has changed since the time you were in school and to recognize the limits of information typically communicated through electronic gradebooks and report cards. Furthermore, we hope you have a greater appreciation for the information communicated through standards-based gradebooks and report cards and are better able to identify how 21st-century grading and assessment benefits your student(s). All the while, we are hopeful this parent guide to grading and reporting, including the final set of questions below, has granted you enhanced clarity about what matters for your child inside and outside of the gradebook.

Questions to Ask Students

- Are there any methods of providing feedback, such as those used by coaches, directors, or leaders, that you find helpful in facilitating learning and that could be implemented in the classroom by teachers?
- What do you think your greatest strengths are for learning something new? Why do you feel that way?
- What do you think is the purpose of grades in school?

Questions to Ask Teachers

- What information have you found useful for parents of previous students in your class to know in order to support their learning?
- What are your vision and goals for my child in this content/course?
- Do you have a preferred method for me to contact you if I have questions or need support? Does it change depending on the day of the week?

References

Allensworth, E. A., & Clark, K. (2020). High school GPAs and ACT scores as predictors of college completion: Examining assumptions across high schools. *Educational Researcher, 49*(3), 198–211.

Bachman, H. F., & Boone, B. J. (2022). A multi-tiered approach to family engagement. *Educational Leadership, 80*(1), 58–62.

Baker, D., & LeTendre, G. (2005). *National differences, global similarities: World culture and the future of schooling.* Stanford University Press.

Baird, A. M., & Parayitam, S. (2019). Employers' ratings of importance of skills and competencies college graduates need to get hired: Evidence from the New England region of USA. *Education + Training, 61*(5), 622–34.

Bennett, C. T. (2021). Untested admissions: Examining changes in application behaviors and student demographics under test-optional policies. *American Educational Research Journal.* https://doi.org/10.3102/00028312211003526.

Blauth, E., & Hadjian, S. (2016, April). *Policy spotlight on New England: How selective colleges and universities evaluate proficiency-based high school transcripts: Insights for students and schools.* New England Board of Higher Education. https://files.eric.ed.gov/fulltext/ED590936.pdf.

Bond, L. A. (1995). *Norm-referenced testing and criterion-referenced testing: The differences in purpose, content, and interpretation of results.* Washington, DC: Office of Educational Research and Improvement.

Bound, J., Lovenheim, M. F., & Turner, S. (2010). Why have college completion rates declined? An analysis of changing student preparation and collegiate resources. *American Economic Journal: Applied Economics, 2*(3): 129–57.

Borba M. (2021). *Thrivers: The surprising reasons why some kids struggle and others shine.* G. P. Putnam's Sons.

Brookhart, S. M. (1991). Grading practices and validity. *Educational Measurement: Issues and Practice, 10*(1), 35–36. doi:10.1111/j.1745-3992.1991.tb00182.x.

———. (2011). Starting the conversation about grading. *Educational Leadership, 69*(3), 10–15.

Brookhart, S. M. (2013). Grading. In J. H. McMillan (Ed.), *Sage handbook of research on classroom assessment* (pp. 257–71). Thousand Oaks, CA: Sage.

Brookhart, S. M., Guskey, T. R., Bowers, A. J., McMillan, J. H., Smith, J. K., Smith, L. F., Stevens, M. T., & Welsh, M. E. (2016). A century of grading research: Meaning and value in the most common educational measure. *Review of Educational Research, 86*(4), 803–48.

Brown, A., & Freeman, A. (2022). The highest-paid YouTube stars: MrBeast, Jake Paul, and Markiplier score massive paydays. *Forbes.* https://www.forbes.com/sites/abrambrown/2022/01/14/the-highest-paid-youtube-stars-mrbeast-jake-paul-and-markiplier-score-massive-paydays/?sh=1956eea41aa7.

Brown, P. C., McDaniel, M. A., Roediger, I. H. L., & Marshall, Q. (2014). *Make it stick: The science of successful learning.* The Belknap Press of Harvard University Press.

Buckmiller, T., & Peters, R. (2018). Getting a fair shot? *School Administrator, 75*(2), 22–25.

Buckmiller, T., Townsley, M., & Cooper, R. (2020). Rural high school principals and the challenge of standards-based grading. *Theory and Practice in Rural Education, 10*(1), 92–102.

Burkhardt, A. L. (2020). *Parents' perception of standards-based grading practices versus norm-referenced grading practices* (Publication No. 27836846). [Doctoral dissertation, Wilmington University]. ProQuest Dissertations & Theses Global.

Castro, M., Expósito-Casas, E., López-Martín, E., Lizasoain, L., Navarro-Asencio, E., & Gaviria, J. L. (2015). Parental involvement on student academic achievement: A meta-analysis. *Educational Research Review, 14*, 33–46.

Chen, X. (2016). Remedial course taking at U.S. public 2- and 4-year institutions: Scope, experiences, and outcomes. Washington, DC: U.S. Department of Education. https://nces.ed.gov/pubs2016/2016405.pdf.

Cizek, G. J., Fitzgerald, J. M., & Rachor, R. A. (1996). Teachers' assessment practices: Preparation, isolation, and the kitchen sink. *Educational Assessment, 3*(2), 159–79. https://doi.org/10.1207/s15326977ea0302_3.

Clinedinst, M. (2019). *2019 state of college admission.* National Association for College Admission Counseling. https://nacacnet.org/wp-content/uploads/2022/10/soca2019_all.pdf.

Common Core State Standards. (n.d.) Development process. http://www.corestandards.org/about-the-standards/development-process/.

Council of Chief State School Officers. (2022). State report card requirements. https://ccsso.org/resource-library/state-report-card-requirements.

Covey, S. R. (2020). *The 7 habits of highly effective people: 30th anniversary edition.* Simon & Schuster.

Cross, L. H., & Frary, R. B. (1999). Hodgepodge grading: Endorsed by students and teachers alike. *Applied Measurement in Education, 12*, 53–72. doi:10.1207/s15324818ame1201_4.

Daggett, B. (2022). Preparing students for their future, not our past. *School Administrator.* https://my.aasa.org/AASA/Resources/SAMag/2022/Mar22/Daggett.aspx.

Dance, A. (July 13, 2021). Pencils down: The year pre-college tests went away. *Knowable Magazine.* https://knowablemagazine.org/article/society/2021/college-ad\missions-testing-pros-cons.

Darling-Hammond, L. (2007). Race, inequality, and educational accountability: the irony of "No Child Left Behind." *Race Ethnicity and Education, 10*(3), 245–60.

———. (2014). *Next generation assessment: Moving beyond the bubble test to support 21st century learning.* Jossey-Bass.

———. (2014). Want to close the achievement gap? Close the teaching gap. *American Educator, 38*(14), 14–18.

Dee, T. S., Jacob, B. A., & Schwartz, N. L. (2013). The effects of NCLB on school resources and practices. *Educational Evaluation and Policy Analysis. 20*(10), 1–28.

Denning, J. T., Eide, E. R., Mumford, K. J., Patterson, R. W., & Warnick, M. (2022). Lower bars, higher college GPAs: How grade inflation is boosting college graduation rates. *Education Next, 22*(1), 56–62.

Dettmers, S., Trautwein, U., Lüdtke, O., Kunter, M., & Baumert, J. (2010). Homework works if homework quality is high: Using multilevel modeling to predict the development of achievement in mathematics. *Journal of Educational Psychology, 102*(2), 467–82.

Dueck, M. (2014). *Grading smarter, not harder: Assessment strategies that motivate kids and help them learn.* ASCD.

Dugan, J. (2022). Co-constructing family engagement. *Educational Leadership, 80*(1), 20–26.

Epstein, J.L., & Van Voorhis, F. L. (2001). More than minutes: Teachers roles in designing homework. *Educational Psychologist, 36*(3), 181–93.

Erkens C., Schimmer, T., & Dimich-Vagle, N. (2017). *Essential assessment: Six tenets for bringing hope efficacy and achievement to the classroom.* Solution Tree Press.

Erkens C., Schimmer T., & Dimich N. (2023). *Jackpot!: Nurturing student investment through assessment.* Solution Tree Press.

Esquivel, P. (2021, November 8). Faced with soaring Ds and Fs, schools are ditching the old way of grading. *Los Angeles Times.*

Every Student Succeeds Act. (n.d.). https://www.ed.gov/essa?src=rn.

Finkelstein, I. E. (1913). *The marking system in theory and practice.* Warwick & York.

Fisher, D., Frey, N., & Pumpian, I. (2011). No penalties for practice. *Educational Leadership*, 69(3), 46–51.

Friedman, M. (2022, September 19). Hamden High students contest GPA weighting inequity. *New Haven Register.* https://www.nhregister.com/news/article/Hamden-High-students-slam-GPA-weighting-inequit-17452436.php.

Friedman, T. L., & Mandlebaum, M. (2012). *That used to be us: How America fell behind in the world it invented and how we can come back.* Picador.

Garlick, S. (2022). *The parenting backpack: Strategies and tools to help you parent with confidence.* At the Parenting Place Publishing.

Goldsmith, M. (n.d.). *Try feedforward instead of feedback.* Marshall Goldsmith. https://marshallgoldsmith.com/articles/try-feedforward-instead-feedback.

Goodwin, B., Rouleau, K., Abla, C., Baptiste, K., Gibson, T., & Kimball, M. (2023). *The new classroom instruction that works: the best research-based strategies for increasing student achievement* (3rd ed.). ASCD; McRel International.

Grant, A. (2021). *Think again: the power of knowing what you don't know.* Viking, an imprint of Penguin Random House LLC.

Guskey, T. R. (2000). Grading policies that work against standards . . . and how to fix them. *NASSP Bulletin, 84*(620), 20–29. https://doi.org/10.1177/019263650008462003.

———. (2002). Computerized gradebooks and the myth of objectivity. *Phi Delta Kappan, 83*(10), 775–80. https://doi.org/10.1177/003172170208301013.

———. (2003). *How's my kid doing? A parent's guide to grades, marks and report cards.* Jossey-Bass.

———. (2009). *Practical solutions for serious problems in standards-based grading.* Corwin Press.

———. (2011). Five obstacles to grading reform. *Educational Leadership, 69*(3), 16–21.

———. (2013). The case against percentage grades. *Educational Leadership, 71*(1), 68–72.

———. (2015). *On your mark: Challenging the conventions of grading and reporting.* Solution Tree Press.

———. (2019). Grades versus comments: Research on student feedback. *Phi Delta Kappan, 101*(30).

———. (2021). Undoing the traditions of grading and reporting. *School Administrator, 78*(5), 32–35.

———. (2022). Can grades be an effective form of feedback? *Phi Delta Kappan*, 104(3), 36–41.

Guskey, T. R., & Bailey, J. (2001). *Developing grading and reporting systems for student learning.* Corwin.

Guskey, T. R., & Brookhart, S. M. (2019). *What we know about grading: What works, what doesn't, and what's next.* ASCD.

Guskey, T., Townsley, M., & Buckmiller, T. (2020). The impact of standards-based learning: Tracking high school students' transition to the university. *NASSP Bulletin, 104*(4), 257–69.

Hansen, M. (2021). The U.S. education system isn't giving students what employers need. *Harvard Business Review.* https://hbr.org/2021/05/the-u-s-education-system-isnt-giving-students-what-employers-need.

Henriksen, D., Mishra, P., Creely, E., & Henderson, M. (2021). The role of creative risk taking and productive failure in education and technology futures. *TechTrends, 65*, 602–605. https://doi.org/10.1007/s11528-021-00622-8.

Hochbein, C., & Pollio, M. (2016). Making grades more meaningful. *Phi Delta Kappan, 98*(3), 49–54.

Hough, L. (2019). Follow the dark horse. *Harvard Ed. Magazine.* Retrieved from: https://www.gse.harvard.edu/news/ed/19/08/follow-dark-horse.

Howell, W. (2006). Switching schools? A closer look at parents' initial interest in and knowledge about the choice provisions of No Child Left Behind. *Peabody Journal of Education, 81*(1), 140–79.

Hursh, D. (2007). Exacerbating inequality: The failed promise of the No Child Left Behind Act. *Race Ethnicity and Education, 10*(3), 295–308.

Iowa State University. (2015). Regents approve alternate admissions index. https://www.inside.iastate.edu/article/2015/02/12/regents.

Jerald, C. D. (2009). Defining a 21st century education. Center for Public Education. Retrieved from: http://www.centerforpubliceducation.org/Learn-About/21st-Century/Defin.

Kamenetz, A. (2018, July 24). *The "overparenting" crisis in school and at home.* NPR. https://www.npr.org/sections/ed/2018/07/24/628042168/the-over-parenting-crisis-in-school-and-at-home.

Kim, J. S., & Sunderman, G. L. (2005). Measuring academic proficiency under the No Child Left Behind Act: Implications for educational equity. *Educational Researcher, 34*(8), 3–13.

Kirschenbaum, H., Napier, R., & Simon, S. B. (2021). *Wad-ja-get?: The grading game in American education.* Michigan Publishing.

Klein, A. (2015, April 10). No Child Left Behind: An overview. *Education Week.* https://www.edweek.org/policy-politics/no-child-left-behind-an-overview/2015/04.

Klopfenstein, K., & Lively, K. (2016). Do grade weights promote more advanced course-taking? *Education Finance and Policy, 11*(3), 310–24.

Knight, M., & Cooper, R. (2019). Taking on a new grading system: The interconnected effects of standards-based grading on teaching, learning, assessment, and student behavior. *NASSP Bulletin, 103*(1), 65–92.

Kohn, A. (2011). *Feel-bad education: Contrarian essays on children and schooling.* Beacon.

Kraft, M. A., & Dougherty, S. M. (2013). The effect of teacher–family communication on student engagement: Evidence from a randomized field experiment. *Journal of Research on Educational Effectiveness, 6*(3), 199–222.

Lahey, J. (2015). *The gift of failure: How the best parents learn to let go so their children can succeed.* Harper.

———. (2019, September 10). How to help your child succeed at school. *The New York Times.* https://www.nytimes.com/guides/smarterliving/help-your-child-succeed-at-school.

Link, L. J., & Guskey, T. R. (2022) Is standards-based grading effective? *Theory Into Practice, 61*(4), 406–17. https://doi.org/10.1080/00405841.2022.2107338.

Littky, D., & Grabelle, S. (2004). *The big picture: Education is everyone's business.* ASCD.

Lucido, J. A. (2018). Understanding the test-optional movement. In Buckley, J., Letukas, L., & Wildavsky, B. *Measuring success: Testing, grades, and the future of college admissions.* Johns Hopkins University Press.

Lythcott-Haims, J. (2015). The over-parenting trap: How to avoid "checklisted" childhoods and raise adults. *Time.* Retrieved from: https://time.com/3910020/the-over-parenting-trap-how-to-avoid-checklisted-childhoods-and-raise-adults.

Marzano, R. J. (2006). *Classroom assessment and grading that work.* ASCD.

Marzano, R. J., & Heflebower, T. (2011). Grades that show what students know. *Educational Leadership, 69*(3), 34–39.

Mastery Transcript Consortium. (2021). *Frequently asked questions.* https://mastery.org/what-we-do/faq.

Maxwell, J. C. (2007). *Failing forward: Turning mistakes into stepping stones for success.* HarperCollins.

McClain, C., Vogels, E. A., Perrin, A., Sechopoulous, S., & Rainie, L. (2021). How the internet and technology shape Americans' personal experiences amid COVID-19. Pew Research Center. https://www.pewresearch.org/internet/2021/09/01/how-the-internet-and-technology-shaped-americans-personal-experiences-amid-covid-19/.

McTighe, J., & Ferrara, S. (2021). *Assessing student learning by design: Principles and practices for teachers and school leaders.* Teachers College Press.

Miami University. (2023). *High school GPA recalculation.* https://miamioh.edu/admission-aid/apply/first-year-students/recalculated-gpa.html.

Minock, N. (2021). Va. teachers push back on equity proposal to abolish some grades, late homework penalties. *WJLA.* https://wjla.com/news/crisis-in-the-classrooms/va-teachers-push-back-on-equity-proposal-to-abolish-some-grades-late-homework-penalties.

Mitani, H. (2018). Principals working conditions, job stress, and turnover behaviors under NCLB accountability pressure. *Educational Administration Quarterly, 54*(5), 822–62.

Mosley, T. (2018, December 28). Mental health experts worry digital "Open Grade Books" are stressing kids out. *KQED.* https://www.kqed.org/news/11714761/mental-health-experts-worry-digital-open-grade-books-are-stressing-kids-out.

National Association of Secondary School Principals. (2020). *Class rank, GPA, and grading.* https://www.nassp.org/class-rank-gpa-and-grading/.

National Center for Education Statistics. (2016). *Remedial coursetaking at U.S. public 2- and 4-year institutions: Scope, experience, and outcomes.* U.S. Department of Education, Institute of Education Sciences. Retrieved from https://nces.ed.gov/pubs2016/2016405.pdf.

———. (2022). Price of attending an undergraduate institution. *Condition of Education.* U.S. Department of Education, Institute of Education Sciences. Retrieved from: https://nces.ed.gov/programs/coe/indicator/cua.

Nietzel, M. T. (2021). The number of students taking the ACT dropped 22% this year. *Forbes.* https://www.forbes.com/sites/michaeltnietzel/2021/10/13/the-number-of-students-taking-the-act-dropped-22-this-year.

Nixa Public Schools. (n.d.). Parent resources: Standards-based grading Q & A. https://www.nixapublicschools.net/Page/4415.

O'Connor, K. (2009). *How to grade for learning, K–12* (3rd ed.). Corwin.

———. (2017). *How to grade for learning: Linking grades to standards.* Corwin.

Pham, L. D., Nguyen, T. D., & Springer, M. G. (2021). Teacher merit pay: A meta-analysis. *American Educational Research Journal, 58*(3), 527–66.

Pink, D. H. (2009). *Drive: The surprising truth about what motivates us.* Riverhead.

Popham, W. J. (2020). *Classroom assessment: What teachers need to know* (9th ed.). Pearson.

Portz, J., & Beauchamp, N. (2022). Educational accountability and state ESSA plans. *Educational Policy, 36*(3), 717–47.

Powell, S. D. (2011). *Introduction to middle school* (2nd ed., pp. 246–47). Pearson.

Qarooni, N. (2022). Seeing families as partners in literacy growth. *Educational Leadership, 80*(1), 35–41.

Reeves, D. B. (2004). The case against the zero. *Phi Delta Kappan, 86*(4), 324–25.

Rose, T. (2016). *The end of average: Unlocking our potential by embracing what makes us different.* HarperCollins.

Rush, L. S., & Scherff, L. (2012). Opening the conversation: NCLB 10 years late. *English Education, 44*(2), 91–101.

Ryan, R. M., & Deci, E. L. (2020). Intrinsic and extrinsic motivation from a self-determination theory perspective: Definitions, theory, practices, and future directions. *Contemporary Educational Psychology, 61.* https://doi.org/10.1016/j.cedpsych.2020.101860.

Saunders-Scott, D., Braley, M. B., & Stennes-Spidahl, N. (2018). Traditional and psychological factors associated with academic success: Investigating best predictors of college retention. *Motivation and Emotion, 42,* 459–65.

Sawchuck, S. (2020, April 1). Grading students during the coronavirus crisis: What's the right call? *Education Week.* https://www.edweek.org/teaching-learning/grading-students-during-the-coronavirus-crisis-whats-the-right-call/2020/04.

Schaeffer, K. (2021, July 1). What we know about online learning and the homework gap amid the pandemic. *Pew Research Center.* https://www.pewresearch.org/fact-tank/2021/10/01/what-we-know-about-online-learning-and-the-homework-gap-amid-the-pandemic.

Schimmer, T. (2016). *Grading from the inside out: Bringing accuracy to student assessment through a standards-based mindset.* Solution Tree Press.

Schinske, J., & Tanner, K. (2014). Teaching more by grading less (or differently). *CBE Life Sciences Education 13*(2), 159–66. https://doi.org/10.1187/cbe.cbe-14-03-0054.

Schoemaker, P. J. H. (2011). *Brilliant mistakes: Finding success on the far side of failure.* Wharton Digital Press.

Simpson, R. L., LaCava, P. G., & Graner, P. S. (2004). The No Child Left Behind Act: Challenges and implications for educators. *Intervention in School and Clinic, 40*(2), 67–75.

Shepherd, L. A., Penuel, W. R., & Pellegrino, J. W. (2018). Using learning and motivation theories to coherently link formative assessment, grading practices, and large-scale assessment. *Educational Measurement: Issues and Practice, 37*(1), 21–34.

Smarter Balanced Assessment Consortium. (n.d.). *Smarter balanced assessments*. www.smarterbalanced.org.

Starch, D., & Elliott, E. C. (1912). Reliability of the grading of high-school work in English. *The School Review 20*(7), 442–57.

Stiggins, R. (1997). *But are they learning?: A commonsense parents' guide to assessment and grading in schools.* Assessment Training Institute.

Stewart, V. (2012). *A world-class education: Learning from international models of excellence and innovation.* ASCD.

Strauss, V. (2016). The case for abolishing class rank. *Washington Post*. https://www.washingtonpost.com/news/answer-sheet/wp/2016/12/13/the-case-for-abolishing-class-rank.

Taketa, K. (2020, October 15). San Diego Unified changes grading practices to be equitable, less punitive. *San Diego Union-Tribune*. https://www.sandiegouniontribune.com/news/education/story/2020-10-15/san-diego-unified-changes-grading-protocols-to-be-more-equitable.

Townsley, M. (2013). Redesigning grading—districtwide. *Educational Leadership, 71*(4), 68–71.

———. (2021). Grading in the midst of a pandemic. *School Administrator*, 78(5), 28–31.

Townsley, M., Buckmiller, T., & Cooper, R. (2019). Anticipating a second wave of standards-based grading implementation and understanding the potential barriers: Perceptions of high school principals. *NASSP Bulletin, 103*(4), 281–99.

Townsley, M., & Kunnath, J. (2022). Exploring state department of education grading guidance during COVID-19: A model for future emergency remote learning. *Education Policy Analysis Archives, 30*(163), 1–23.

U.S. Department of Education. (2004). Executive summary. https://www2.ed.gov/nclb/overview/intro/execsumm.html.

Vatterott, C. (2011). Making homework central to learning. *Educational Leadership, 69*(3), 60–64.

———. (2015). *Rethinking grading: Meaningful assessment for standards-based learning.* ASCD.

Vickers, J. M. (2000). Justice and truth in grades and their averages. *Research in Higher Education, 41*, 141–64.

Wagner, T., & Bhatt, S. G. (2021). "Innovation-ready" graduates. *School Administrator*, 9(78), 24–29.

Warne, R. T., Nagaishi, C., Slade, M. K., Hermesmeyer, P., & Peck, E. K. (2014). Comparing weighted and unweighted grade point averages in predicting college success of diverse and low income students. *NASSP Bulletin, 98*(4), 261–79.

Wiggins, G. (2002, January 21). Toward genuine accountability: The case for a new state assessment system. George Lucas Educational Foundation: *Edutopia*. https://www.edutopia.org/toward-genuine-accountability-case-new-state-assessment-system.

Winstead, L. (2011). The impact of NCLB and accountability on social studies: Teacher experiences and perceptions about teaching social studies. *The Social Studies, 102*(5), 221–27.

Wisch, J., Ousterhout, B., Carter, V., & Orr, B. (2018). The grading gradient: Teacher motivations for varied redo and retake policies. *Studies in Educational Evaluation, 58*, 145–55.

Wormeli, R. (2006). *Fair isn't always equal: Assessing & grading in the differentiated classroom.* Stenhouse Publishers.

———. (2011). Redos and retakes done right. *Educational Leadership, 69*(3), 22–26.

———. (2014). Motivating young adolescents. *Educational Leadership, 72*(1), 26–31.

Woodinville High School. (n.d.). https://woodinville.nsd.org/counseling/grading-report-cards.

Zaloom, C. (2019). *Indebted: How families make college work at any cost.* Princeton University Press.

Index

accountability, student: academic and non-academic factors in, 34–35; apathy rewarding concern addressed for, 36; grading and student motivation, 44–46; measures, 2; perils of carrot-and-stick approach, 44–46; problem with zeros and, 36, 38–42; redos, retakes and, 35–38; sample schoolwide descriptors of learning, *41*; understanding 21st-century grading and, 34

ACT exams: class rank and, 53; college completion and, 56; SAT and, 22, 53

Adams, Sherry, gradebook of, 18, *18*

advanced placement courses, 49–50, 51

Amanda (parent of 8th grader), 66–67

assessment: ACT exam, 22, 53, 56; criterion-referenced, 22; defined, 20; ESSA, 4–5; literacy, 60; norm-referenced, 22; purposes of 21st century, 61; role of standards in, *21*; SAT, 22, 53; standardized tests implemented for, 3; timeframes, 38; traditional v. modern expectations in, *29*. *See also* reassessment

averages, problem with basing grades on, 42–43, *43*. *See also* grade point average

Bartell family scenario, 17

Ben (high school student), 49–50

big picture, x, 67–71

big red book, 12

Canady, Robert, 42

career readiness: factory model in past, 29; grading and, 23; homework as "practice" for, 23–27; non-college pathway to, 55–56; standardized assessments and, 23

carrot-and-stick approach, 44–46, 68

Carson, Rachel, 68

category weighting setup, gradebook, *41*

children: disillusionment in, 71; feelings, love of learning in, 68; mental health of, 14

college: admission, 53–56; Bartell family scenario, 17; completion, 19, 56; cost increase, 54–55; GPAs, class rank and, 50–53; high school Advanced Placement courses and, 49–50; remedial courses in, 55; scholarships, 53; student challenges in, 17–18

Common Core State Standards, 3

communication: do and don't example of parent-teacher, 65; feedforward, 70; "outside" triad, 66–67; traditional parent-teacher, 64

communication triad, student-parent-teacher, 60; communicating "outside" of, 66–67; note of caution for, 65; parents busy lives and need for, 67–68; for successful students, 62–66, *64*

completion, learning v., 13, 65. *See also* college

conduct, grades based on attitude and, 19

confirmation bias, 45

consolidation, in memory and brain function, 69

content areas, on standards-based report cards, 8

Covey, Stephen, 46

COVID-19 pandemic: criterion-referenced assessment and, 22; fallout from, xiv; homework during early years of, 24–25; 21st-century grading and, 11–12, 27

credits, for non-learning activities, 19

criterion-referenced assessments, 22

curriculums: moving target of, 28; teaching model in traditional, 28. *See also* extracurricular activities personnel, communication and

Daggett, Bill, 55
David Douglas School District, standards-based report card, 9–11
deadlines, 34–35
Dede, Christopher, ix
deep learning, 29–30
descriptors, of learning, 40, *41*
Donald, gradebooks of Susan and, 40–42, *41*

economy, skills needed in gig, 30
education, changing landscape of, 2–5
Einstein, Albert, 71
electronic gradebooks: perils of "scoreboard watching" and, 12–14; real-time communication in online, 38; software applications for reading, 12
Eliza (student nervous about math), 66–67
emotions, knowledge and, 68
employees, skills of students v., 25–26
English language arts, 21st-century assessment example, *29*
Every Student Succeeds Act (ESSA), 4–5
extracurricular activities personnel, communication and, 66–67

Failing Forward (Maxwell), 68
failure: learning from, 69; permission for, 68–69
feedback, communicating about style of, 66–67
feedforward communication, 70

"get it done at all costs" model, 24
The Gift of Failure (Lahey), 14, 66
gig economy, 30
Goldsmith, Marshall, 70
GPA. *See* grade point average
gradebooks, 40–42; category weighting setup, *41*; hodgepodge, *18*; percentage-based setup, *41*; problems with averaging shown in sample, *43*. *See also* electronic gradebooks
gradebooks, standards-based, 1, 5, 15; dynamic nature of, 7; perils of electronic gradebooks, 12–14; sample for 8th-grade science student, 6–7, *8*
grade point average (GPA), 49; class rank and, 50–53; college completion link with, 56; high school transcripts containing letter grades and, 54; sample unweighted scale for, *51*; sample weighted scale for, *52*; variations between high schools, 51–52
grades: "earned," 71; hyper focus on completion and, 65; as merely indicators, 71; survey on purpose of, 71; traditional view of as mystery, 71
grading: average-based, 42–43, *43*; career readiness and, 23; descriptors of learning, 40, *41*; hodgepodge, *18*, 18–20, 23, 28; in industrial model, 29; parents confirmation bias regarding, 45; problem with homework included in, 25–26, 69; student motivation and, 44–46. *See also* traditional grading; 21st-century grading
Guskey, Thomas, 19

Harvard Ed. Magazine, 45
high schools: advanced placement courses in, 49–50; class rank in, 52; GPA variations between, 51–52; letter grades continuing in, 53–54; physical education in, 51–52; positioning, 49–50
hodgepodge grading: career readiness and, 23; "kitchen sink" and, *18*, 18–20; as outdated, 28
home progress reports, 13
homework: averaging practice with mastery and, 26; final grade not including, 25; "get it done at all costs" model, 24; late work and, 34, 36; as "practice," 23–27; problem with grading inclusion of, 25–26; quality, 25

IB. *See* International Baccalaureate
Indebted (Zaloom), 55
industrial revolution, 29
Infinite Campus, 12
International Baccalaureate (IB), 51

jobs, requirements for 21st century, 28
Jones family scenario, x, 1, 13, 14–15

kindergarten, making mistakes and, 68
Kirshenbaum, Howard, 71
Kohn, Alfie, 34, 52

Lahey, Jessica, 14, 66
language of learning, 70
late work: consequences of rejecting, 36; not penalizing students for, 34
learning: assessment definition and, 20; change in type of, 27–30; completion v., 13, 65; deep, 29–30; descriptors of, 40, *41*; extrinsic rewards for, 44; Guskey on misrepresentations

of, 19; idea behind essential, 45–46; language of, 70; love of, 68; proficiency scales, *62*; proficiency tools, 61, *62*; recency of, 42–44; remote, 11–12; transparency in, 60–62; "work" and, x. *See also* levels of learning
learning progression scale, 59
letter grades: high schools as continuing to give, 53–54; one-dimensional view of, 71; percentage scale compared to, *39*; state choice to use, 7–8; typical grading scale using, *39*
levels of learning: communicating, 8, 12–14; standards-based report card, *9–11*

mastery, averaging practice with, 26
Mastery Transcript Consortium (MTC), 50, 54
math: 8th grader needing more feedback in, 66–67; 21st-century assessment example, *29*
Maxwell, John C., 68
memorization, x, 3
mental health, of child: scoreboard watching impact on, 14
minimum proficiency, 59
mistakes: conversations about failures and, 70; early childhood, kindergarten and, 68; engineering, 69
modern proficiency expectations, traditional v., *29*
motivation: grading and student, 44–46; intrinsic, 36, 65
MTC. *See* Mastery Transcript Consortium
"mulligans," 37
Murphy, David (divorced father of 6th grader), 59–60

NACAC. *See* National Association for College Admission Counseling
Napier, Rodney, 71
National Association for College Admission Counseling (NACAC), 53
National Association of Secondary School Principals, 52–53
NCLB. *See* No Child Left Behind Act
New England Board of Higher Education, 54
New England Secondary School Consortium, 54
No Child Left Behind Act (NCLB), 2; critics of, 3–4; ESSA as replacing, 4; local variations and expectations prior to, 3
norm-referenced assessments, 22
NPR interview, with teacher, 66

O'Connor, Ken, 36
omnibus grading. *See* hodgepodge grading

parents/guardians: areas of help for, xv; assessment literacy of, 60; big picture view for, 67–71; changing mindset towards grades, 70; communication between community and, 66–67; completion-focused, 65; partnership with, ix; using grades like currency, 65; yearly goals and, 68
partnership, xv; parent-school, ix; parent-student, 59–60
PE. *See* physical education
percentage-based setup, gradebook, *41*
percentage scale: letter grades compared to, *39*; traditional grade letter performance levels and, *40*
perfection, push for, 69
permission, to fail, 68
physical education (PE), 51–52; sample single-point rubric for middle school, *62*
PowerSchool, 12
practice, averaging mastery with, 26
procrastination, 36
progress reports, home, 13
push for perfection, trend of, 69

questions: end-of-chapter reflective, xvi; on standardized tests, 3, *3*

RAI. *See* Regents Admissions Index
real-world implications, of 21st-century grading: academic/non-academic factors and, 34–35; full credit for redos and retakes in, 35–38; grading and student motivation, 44–46; perils of carrot-and-stick approach, 44–46
reassessment, 36–37, *37*
recalculation scales, at some colleges, 52
redo policy, 36
Regents Admissions Index (RAI), 52–53
report cards: 6th-grader conversation with father about, 59–60; standards-based, 8, *9–11*
Rose, Todd, 45

Santa Rosa Elementary School, performance profile, *4–6*
SAT exams: ACT and, 22, 53; college completion and, 56
SBG. *See* standards-based gradebooks; standards-based grading
scenarios: advanced placement courses (Ben), 49–50; Amanda (parent of 8th grader), 66–67; Bartell family, 17; divorced father of 6th grader, 59–60; Eliza (nervous math student), 66–67; gradebook of Adams, Sherry, 18, *18*;

gradebooks of Susan and Donald, 40–42, *41*; Jones family, x, 1, 13, 14–15
scholarships, 53
schools: accountability measures, 2; changes in K–12, xiv; performance metrics requirement for, 4, *4*; post-COVID-19 flexibility in, 12
science, assessment example for, *29*
scoreboard watching, xv; perils of, 12–14
The Sense of Wonder (Carson), 68
The 7 Habits of Highly Effective People (Covey), 46
Simon, Sidney, 71
skills, needed by students, x, 45; employability, 34, 55–56; in gig economy, 30; non-academic, 23, 35; required for 21st-century jobs, 28; student v. employee, 25–26
Skyward, 12
Smarter Balanced Assessments Consortium, 3
Smith family scenario, 33
snapshot analogy, for assessment, 20
social studies: sample 4th-grade proficiency scale in, *62*; 21st-century assessment example, *29*
software applications, 12
Sophie (6th grader), conversation with father about report card, 59–60
standardized assessments: *assessments* defined, 20; career readiness implications of, 23; controversial nature of, 20–21; tradition v. digital, 20
standardized tests: questions on, 3; state-by-state and common, 3
standards: assessment role of, *21*; content areas and, 8; report cards based on, 8, *9–11*; state, 3; *targets* and, 5
standards-based gradebooks (SBG), 1, 5; dynamic nature of, 7; perils of electronic gradebooks, 12–14; sample for 8th-grade science student, 6–7, *8*
state standards, 3
Stiggins, Rick, 45
students: communication triad for successful, 62–64; grading and motivation, 44–46; as learners, not future adults, 34; skills needed by, x; skills of employees v., 25–26. *See also* accountability, student

targets, standards and, 5
teachers. *See* communication triad, student-parent-teacher; partnership
tests. *See* assessment; standardized tests
traditional curriculums, 28
traditional grading, xiv, 12; "final grade" in, 42; grade letter performance levels and percentage scale, *40*; hodgepodge, *18*, 18–20, 23, 28; modern proficiency expectations v., *29*; perils of carrot-and-stick approach in, 44–46, 68; progress reports and, 13; push for perfection in, 69; variation between teachers, 30
transparency, 60–62
21st-century grading: academic and non-academic factors separated in, 34–35; aims of, 53; benefit of understanding, xiv–xv; benefits of, 14–15; COVID-19 Pandemic and, 11–12, 27; homework in, 25; implications, xv; intent of, 1; letter grades choice in, 7–8; letters or numbers used in, 8–9; names of example, ix; rationale, xv; real-world implications of, 34–44; terminology and, xiii, xvi; traditional v., *29*, *39*, 46; transition to, ix; as umbrella term, xiii, xvi. *See also* assessment; real-world implications, of 21st-century grading; traditional grading practices

Wad-Ja-Get? The Grading Game in American Education (Kirshenbaum, Napier, Simon), 71
Whitaker, Todd, 65–66
Wiggins, Grant, 20
work: consequences of rejecting, 36; late, 34; substituting "learning" for "work," x
Wormeli, Rick, 36

YouTubers, 55

Zaloom, Caitlin, 55
zeros, problem with, 36, 38–42

About the Authors

Matt Townsley, EdD, is an assistant professor of educational leadership at the University of Northern Iowa in Cedar Falls, Iowa. As a former district administrator and teacher in the Solon Community School District (Solon, IA), he has firsthand experience implementing and leading lasting grading reform. *District Administration* magazine named Solon Community Schools a district of distinction, and Solution Tree recognized multiple buildings in the district as model professional learning communities during his tenure. Through conferences, professional development, and workshops, Dr. Townsley has consulted with thousands of educators and parents across the globe on the topics of assessment and grading.

In 2017, Dr. Townsley was named Iowa's Central Office Administrator of the year and in 2014, he was recognized as an ASCD Emerging Leader. He has authored multiple books, including *Making Grades Matter: Standards-Based Grading in a Secondary PLC at Work* (2020, Solution Tree) and *Using Grading to Support Student Learning* (2022). Dr. Townsley's writing can be found in practitioner-oriented publications such as *Educational Leadership*, *School Administrator*, and *ASCD Express* as well as research journals such as *NASSP Bulletin*, *Journal of School Leadership,* and *American Secondary Education*. In addition, he has been featured or quoted on or in *The Christian Science Monitor*, CNN.com, the *Washington Post*, California and Kansas public radio, the Center for Digital Education, *Education Week*, Khan Academy Ed Talks, and presented at national conferences such as the Learning Forward Annual Conference, National Conference on Education (AASA), and the Association for Middle Level Education (AMLE) Annual Conference.

Dr. Townsley holds a bachelor's degree in mathematics education from Wartburg College, a master's degree in curriculum and instructional technology from Iowa State University, a certificate of advanced studies in educational leadership from the University of Northern Iowa, and a doctorate in school improvement from the University of West Georgia.

To learn more about his work, visit www.mctownsley.net or follow @mctownsley on Twitter/X.

Chad Lang, EdD, is the Assistant Superintendent of School Improvement and Human Resources at Glenwood Community School District in Glenwood, Iowa. Dr. Lang has extensive PK–12 experience, having served as a high school teacher and coach, assistant middle school principal, and district activities director. With nearly two decades of experience in teaching and school leadership, Dr. Lang has a deep understanding of grading reform and its importance in 21st-century education. He has firsthand experience implementing grading reform as a teacher in Missouri and administrator in Iowa, where he leads district training and implementation.

Throughout his career, Dr. Lang has received numerous accolades from students, peers, and professional associations. These include the Excelsior Springs High School's (Excelsior Springs, Missouri) "Teacher I Never Want to Miss" and "Most Challenging Teacher" Awards in 2011, 2023 Iowa Central Office Administrator of the Year, and the Missouri State Athletic Director of the Year (MIAAA) in 2018. Dr. Lang has a wealth of experience teaching high school social studies, having taught in Iowa, Missouri, and abroad in the St. Croix Virgin Islands, as well as virtually to Brazilian students. Additionally, he currently serves as an adjunct professor in the graduate school of education at the University of Nebraska-Omaha.

Dr. Lang's research areas include grading and assessment, extracurricular participation, and school leadership. His work has been featured in various publications, such as *Educational Leadership*, *Phi Delta Kappan*, *Journal of School Administration Research and Development*, and *Theory & Practice in Rural Education*. He has also been a speaker at conferences, including the Ignite Leadership Virtual Summit in 2021, the Missouri Athletic Director's Annual Conference in 2018, and the Missouri Association of Secondary School Principals Conference in 2016.

Dr. Lang received his bachelor's degree in social science education from the University of Northern Iowa, a master's degree in secondary school administration from William Woods University, and a doctorate of educational leadership and policy analysis from the University of Missouri-Columbia.

You can follow Dr. Lang's work on Twitter/X at @Chad_mLang.

www.ingramcontent.com/pod-product-compliance
Lightning Source LLC
Chambersburg PA
CBHW081846230426
43669CB00018B/2841